T5-DHH-301

Boston University

Boston, Massachusetts

Written by Caren Walker

*Edited by Adam Burns, Meghan Dowdell,
and Kimberly Moore*

Layout by Meghan Dowdell

ISBN # 1-4274-0024-5
ISSN # 1551-9546
© Copyright 2006 College Prowler
All Rights Reserved
Printed in the U.S.A.
www.collegeprowler.com

Last updated 9/12/07

Special thanks to: Babs Carryer, Andy Hannah, LaunchCyte, Tim O'Brien, Bob Sehlinger, Thomas Emerson, Andrew Skurman, Barbara Skurman, Bert Mann, Dave Lehman, Daniel Fayock, Chris Babyak, The Donald H. Jones Center for Entrepreneurship, Terry Slease, Jerry McGinnis, Bill Ecenberger, Idie McGinty, Kyle Russell, Jacque Zaremba, Larry Winderbaum, Roland Allen, Jon Reider, Team Evankovich, Lauren Varacalli, Abu Noaman, Jason Putorti, Mark Exler, Daniel Steinmeyer, Jared Cohon, Gabriela Oates, David Koegler, and Glen Meakem.

Bounce-Back Team: Benjamin Cassou, Michele Kligman, and Melissa Auerbach

College Prowler®
5001 Baum Blvd.
Suite 750
Pittsburgh, PA 15213

Phone: 1-800-290-2682
Fax: 1-800-772-4972
E-Mail: info@collegeprowler.com
Web Site: www.collegeprowler.com

College Prowler® is not sponsored by, affiliated with, or approved by Boston University in any way.

College Prowler® strives faithfully to record its sources. As the reader understands, opinions, impressions, and experiences are necessarily personal and unique. Accordingly, there are, and can be, no guarantees of future satisfaction extended to the reader.

© Copyright 2006 College Prowler. All rights reserved. No part of this work may be reproduced or transmitted in any form or by any means, including but not limited to, photocopy, recording, or any information storage and retrieval systems, without the express written permission of College Prowler®.

How this all started...

When I was trying to find the perfect college, I used every resource that was available to me. I went online to visit school websites; I talked with my high school guidance counselor; I read book after book; I hired a private counselor. Sure, this was all very helpful, but nothing really told me what life was like at the schools I cared about. These sources weren't giving me enough information to be totally confident in my decision.

In all my research, there were only two ways to get the information I wanted.

The first was to physically visit the campuses and see if things were really how the brochures described them, but this was quite expensive and not always feasible. The second involved a missing ingredient: the students. Actually talking to a few students at those schools gave me a taste of the information that I needed so badly. The problem was that I wanted more but didn't have access to enough people.

In the end, I weighed my options and decided on a school that felt right and had a great academic reputation, but truth be told, the choice was still very much a crapshoot. I had done as much research as any other student, but was I 100 percent positive that I had picked the school of my dreams?

Absolutely not.

My dream in creating *College Prowler* was to build a resource that people can use with confidence. My own college search experience taught me the importance of gaining true insider insight; that's why the majority of this guide is composed of quotes from actual students. After all, shouldn't you hear about a school from the people who know it best?

I hope you enjoy reading this book as much as I've enjoyed putting it together. Tell me what you think when you get a chance. I'd love to hear your college selection stories.

Luke Skurman
CEO and Co-Founder
lukeskurman@collegeprowler.com

Welcome to College Prowler®

During the writing of College Prowler's guidebooks, we felt it was critical that our content was unbiased and unaffiliated with any college or university. We think it's important that our readers get honest information and a realistic impression of the student opinions on any campus—that's why if any aspect of a particular school is terrible, we (unlike a campus brochure) intend to publish it. While we do keep an eye out for the occasional extremist—the cheerleader or the cynic—we take pride in letting the students tell it like it is. We strive to create a book that's as representative as possible of each particular campus. Our books cover both the good and the bad, and whether the survey responses point to recurring trends or a variation in opinion, these sentiments are directly and proportionally expressed through our guides.

College Prowler guidebooks are in the hands of students throughout the entire process of their creation. Because you can't make student-written guides without the students, we have students at each campus who help write, randomly survey their peers, edit, layout, and perform accuracy checks on every book that we publish. From the very beginning, student writers gather the most up-to-date stats, facts, and inside information on their colleges. They fill each section with student quotes and summarize the findings in editorial reviews. In addition, each school receives a collection of letter grades (A through F) that reflect student opinion and help to represent contentment, prominence, or satisfaction for each of our 20 specific categories. Just as in grade school, the higher the mark the more content, more prominent, or more satisfied the students are with the particular category.

Once a book is written, additional students serve as editors and check for accuracy even more extensively. Our bounce-back team—a group of randomly selected students who have no involvement with the project—are asked to read over the material in order to help ensure that the book accurately expresses every aspect of the University and its students. This same process is applied to the 200-plus schools College Prowler currently covers. Each book is the result of endless student contributions, hundreds of pages of research and writing, and countless hours of hard work. All of this has led to the creation of a student information network that stretches across the nation to every school that we cover. It's no easy accomplishment, but it's the reason that our guides are such a great resource.

When reading our books and looking at our grades, keep in mind that every college is different and that the students who make up each school are not uniform—as a result, it is important to assess schools on a case-by-case basis. Because it's impossible to summarize an entire school with a single number or description, each book provides a dialogue, not a decision, that's made up of 20 different topics and hundreds of student quotes. In the end, we hope that this guide will serve as a valuable tool in your college selection process. Enjoy!

OMID GOHARI ○ CHRISTINA KOSHZOW ○ CHRIS MASON ○ JOEY RAHIMI ○ LUKE SKURMAN ○
The College Prowler Team

BOSTON UNIVERSITY

Table of Contents

Introduction from the Author

You are about to embark on an all-inclusive, first-person report on Boston University. If you are reading this introduction, it means that you probably already have some interest in BU, and you were inspired to consider it as an option for furthering your education. It is my job, in the following pages, to give you some insight about BU.

So, what is my perspective? I am writing as a recent graduate (read: unemployed) from this fine institution, with a double degree in philosophy and psychology from the College of Arts and Sciences. I have lived in Boston, both on and off campus, for the past four years, and have a pretty good idea of the resources—and frustrations —you will stumble upon, assuming that you decide to attend. Unlike many of the post-adolescent, idealistically-oriented cynics I spend most of my time with, I have actually engaged in BU life and academia enough to report back to you in an honest, and even optimistic, fashion. The purpose of the following is to provide you with a fairly entertaining, and hopefully coherent stream of consciousness as I reflect on my college experience. Allow me to elaborate.

Boston University has a reputation that generally holds true when considering the students, faculty, and administrative aspects of university life. While the University is a huge community, it is possible and necessary to establish yourself as an individual entity and independently-thinking being, despite the obvious obstacles. For those of you who are hesitant to leave high school behind, you are in good company. I am currently in the position of dealing with the same sort of confusion and instability in prying myself away from college life. To put things in perspective: you have nothing to worry about. College will be one of the most dramatic learning experiences of your life, if you allow it to be. This place, both the good and the bad, has played a huge role in my perception of the "real world."

The truth: college is a time during which you exist each day, liberated from the confines of life, while remaining cared for and sheltered on a very necessary level. Considering that college is such a huge transition, choosing a school certainly has undeniable effects on the course of your near and distant future. On the other hand, most universities, especially those offering as large a community as BU, will probably be equally enabling to your self-actualization. Nevertheless, the following information and suggestions should make the overwhelming nature of the process of starting school slightly less paralyzing.

Caren M. Walker, Author
Boston University, College of Arts and Sciences

By the Numbers

General Information

Boston University
881 Commonwealth Avenue
Boston, Massachusetts 02215

Control:
Private

Academic Calendar:
Semester

Religious Affiliation:
None

Founded:
1839

Web Site:
www.bu.edu

Main Phone:
(617) 353-2000

Admissions Phone:
(617) 353-2300

Student Body

**Full-Time
Undergraduates:**
16,386

**Part-Time
Undergraduates:**
1,354

**Total Male
Undergraduates:**
7,279

**Total Female
Undergraduates:**
10,461

Admissions

Overall Acceptance Rate:
55%

Early Decision Acceptance Rate:
47%

Regular Acceptance Rate:
56%

Total Applicants:
28,240

Total Acceptances:
15,660

Freshman Enrollment:
4,352

Yield (% of admitted students who actually enroll):
27.8%

Early Decision Available?
Yes

Early Action Available?
No

Early Decision Deadline:
November 1

Early Decision Notification:
December 15

Regular Decision Deadline:
January 1

Regular Decision Notification:
Mid March–mid April

Must-Reply-By Date:
May 1

Applicants Placed on Waiting List:
1,738

Applicants Accepted from Waiting List:
833

Students Enrolled from Waiting List:
1,717

Transfer Applications Received:
1,829

Transfer Applications Accepted:
637

Transfer Students Enrolled:
234

Transfer Application Acceptance Rate:
35%

Common Application Accepted?
Yes

Supplemental Forms?
Essay of no longer than 500 words

Admissions E-Mail:
admissions@bu.edu

Admissions Web Site:
www.bu.edu/admission

SAT I or ACT Required?
Either

SAT I Range (25th–75th Percentile):
1210–1390

**SAT I Verbal Range
(25th–75th Percentile):**
600–690

**SAT I Math Range
(25th–75th Percentile):**
610–700

SAT II Requirements:
For all applicants, the Writing
and Foreign Language tests
are recommended; for the
Accelerated Medical and
Accelerated Dental Programs,
Chemistry, Mathematics Level
IIc, and Writing are required,
and a Foreign Language test is
strongly recommended.

Retention Rate:
89%

**Top 10% of
High School Class:**
60%

**Top 25% of
High School Class:**
90%

**Top 50% of
High School Class:**
100%

Application Fee:
$70

Financial Information

Tuition:
$31,966 per year

Part-Time Tuition:
$845 per credit
(most classes are 4 credits)

Room and Board:
$10,080

Books and Supplies:
$754 per year

**Average Need-Based
Financial Aid Package
(including loans, work-study,
grants, and other sources):**
$17,748

**Students Who
Applied for Financial Aid:**
51%

Students Who Received Aid:
More than $173.4 million
granted to 12,087 students
who applied and received
financial aid, 46%

Financial Aid Forms Deadline:
February 15

Financial Aid Phone:
(617) 353-2965

Financial Aid E-Mail:
finaid@bu.edu

Financial Aid Web Site:
www.bu.edu/finaid

Academics

The Lowdown On...
Academics

Degrees Awarded:
Bachelor
Master
Doctorate

Most Popular Majors:
18% Communications, Journalism
17% Business, Management, Marketing, Support Services
16% Social Sciences
8% Psychology
7% Engineering

Undergraduate Schools:
College of Arts and Sciences
College of Communication
College of Engineering
College of General Studies
Goldman School of Dental Medicine
School of Education
School of Hospitality Administration
School of Management
School of Medicine
University Professors Program

➜

Full-Time Faculty:
2,338

Total Faculty:
3,410

Faculty with Terminal Degree:
83%

Student-to-Faculty Ratio:
13:1

Average Course Load:
16 credits (4 courses)

Graduation Rate:
Four-Year: 62%
Five-Year: 73%
Six-Year: 75%

Special Degree Options
Several dual degrees are offered as double majors within colleges of the University. BUCOP—the Boston University Collaborative Degree Program (dual degrees awarded between colleges within the University); five-year BA/MA program in the College of Arts and Sciences; five-year MBA program in the School of Management; seven-year liberal arts/medical education program offers the BA and MD; and a seven-year liberal arts/dental education program offers the BA and DMD; the College of Arts and Sciences and the School of Medicine jointly offer the eight-year Modular Medical Integrated Curriculum (MMEDIC), leading to a BA and MD.

AP Test Score Requirements
Possible credit for scores of 3, 4, or 5, depending on specific requirements of the program.

IB Test Score Requirements
Possible credit and/or placement; call (617) 353-4492 for more information on IB.

Did You Know?

The Core Curriculum Program is an option for the top candidates entering the College of Arts and Sciences, and an excellent opportunity for those of us lacking specific direction or major. Core consists of eight historically-based, integrated courses providing an in-depth study of classic works in the humanities, natural sciences, and social sciences. While Core does emphasize a higher ability for analytical thinking, and certainly requires higher levels of writing and reading comprehension than other programs, it allows students to pursue a coherent interdisciplinary approach to literature, art, music, social, religious, scientific, and philosophical thought, therefore enabling you to sound extra-intelligent at social gatherings and heated debates. Core lectures are always accompanied by small seminar discussions and labs, so get ready for a rocky time at registration. Beware, scheduling around Core classes can prove to be difficult.

BU Was the First to:

- Open all its divisions to women (1872)
- Open a college of music in the United States (1873)
- Admit women to its medical college, the School of Medicine (1873)
- To award PhDs to women in America (1877)
- Offer a college degree in public relations (1947)
- Open a graduate school in dentistry (1963)
- Combine cancer research and a teaching laboratory (1965)

Best Places to Study:

The George Sherman Union is always a favorite place. Of course, we mourn the loss of the smoking lounge, which has fallen as a casualty of a more health-conscious nation. The "BU Beach," which acquired its name due to the sound of the "rushing" traffic against the "shore," is one of the few grassy areas on campus and is always filled with students during good weather.

Students Speak Out On...
Academics

"As a freshman, you will have huge lectures, and depending on your major, that might not change too much. The teachers are brilliant, but you might get lost in the crowd."

Q "Generally, I liked my teachers. **The chemistry department is awesome**, but I didn't like my first taste of the biology department. The lectures are large, but other classes, such as my French and writing classes, usually consisted of about 20 people."

Q "**The teachers are there if you need them**. It's what you make of it. If you go to them for help they are usually happy to talk to you. If you don't make a point of going to their office hours and allowing them the opportunity to learn your name, they might know you only as a number."

Q "A lot of classes are lectures, so you don't have any one-on-one time with your professors. But if you go to their office hours, **they usually love to meet with students and will help you out**. Some professors aren't so much interested in teaching as in hearing themselves talk, but it's like that at all colleges, unfortunately."

Q "I hear that BU has some of the top professors around (Elie Wiesel, for example, teaches classes in the University Professors, theology, and Core), but **the most renowned professors aren't very accessible**. It's a big school, and that's just the way it is. But I have had some excellent professors who really care about their students, and they are very available. Some of the grad students aren't that bad either, and they can be very good resources."

Q "Freshman year, you'll have at least one class that is small—a writing class with 15-25 people in it. Other than that, most of the 100-level classes are large. The TFs (teaching fellows) are always glad to help out, but they don't teach the class, and sometimes **they don't speak English very well**."

Q "The professors are mostly the same; they all love learning about their subject, and some even like teaching it, too. Usually it's the same deal, but at least once a year, you'll find a great teacher. Furthermore, most people would assume that taking required classes sucks, and yes, in fact, it does suck, but fortunately they're at least somewhat appealing—sometimes even fascinating—even if you don't care for the subject. Honestly, I think the whole idea of a Core curriculum is generally whack, but ironically, my Core classes really weren't that bad. And even though I didn't really do too well on the test, I still enjoyed most of the classes overall, and in the end, I'd say **I learned a lot of interesting things, too**."

Q "What's most important about enjoying a class and professor at BU is getting past the 101 and introductory courses (most of them are so darn broad, and they pretty much suck). Once you get more specific with regards to your personal interests, classes become much more enjoyable. I found it difficult, though, to get a good rapport with the professors I enjoyed and respected, simply **because the majority of the classes were so huge**. It's helpful to ask around and get some feedback before you take a potential class with a particular professor in order to see what other students had to say about him or her."

The College Prowler Take On...
Academics

As with any university, the nature of the classes is largely dependent on the particular professors teaching them. Everyone seems to agree that the best way to choose a class is by first learning about the professor's teaching style from other students. While some professors fall into anonymity after the last day of class, some directly influence the course of your education. Don't get frustrated with your 100-level introductory classes; they are universally described as "a waste of time," "boring," and "impersonal." Get through your requirements, but keep in mind that the best classes are the upper-levels.

As it happened, I was so inspired by a particular professor during my sophomore year, that I decided to become a psych major—only to find out later that it was the individual himself, not the field, that held my interest. Those types of professors, while few and far between, are certainly present and available to any student who seeks them out.

The College Prowler® Grade on
Academics: B+

A high Academics grade generally indicates that professors are knowledgeable, accessible, and genuinely interested in their students' welfare. Other determining factors include class size, how well professors communicate, and whether or not classes are engaging.

Local Atmosphere

The Lowdown On...
Local Atmosphere

Region:
New England

City, State:
Boston, Massachusetts

Setting:
City

Distance from NYC:
4 hours

Closest Shopping Malls:
CambridgeSide Galleria
Copley Mall
Harvard Square
Prudential Center

Major Sports Teams:
Red Sox (baseball)
Bruins (hockey)
Celtics (basketball)
Patriots (football)

Points of Interest:

Boston Commons

Boston Pops

Boston Public Gardens

Boston Symphony Orchestra

Chinatown

Contemporary Art

Faneuil Hall Marketplace

Fenway Park

Freedom Trail

Isabella Stewart Gardner Museum

Museum of Fine Arts and Museum of Science

New England Aquarium (with IMAX)

Newbury Street

Quincy Market and

The Charles River

The Institute for

The North End

Closest Movie Theaters:

AMC Fenway
201 Brookline Ave.
Boston, MA 02215
(617) 424-6266

Copley Theatre
100 Huntington Ave.
Boston, MA 02116
(617) 266-1300

Loews Boston Commons
75 Tremont St.
Boston, MA 02111
(617) 423-3499

Coolidge Corner
(mostly independent films)
290 Harvard St.
Brookline, MA 02446
(617) 734-2501

City Web Sites

www.boston.com will give you all of the info and links
you need to keep up with local news, entertainment, and
restaurant listings. Any Boston information not on the Web site
can probably be easily accessed through one of the links listed
at this site. Also, check out *www.bostonvisit.com*.

Did You Know?

Go to the MIT museum. It is an interactive, hands-on museum displaying Artificial Intelligence, Hall of Holograms, Mechanical Artwork, and other really incredible exhibits. Best of all, it is only $2 to get in with your student ID.

5 Fun Facts about Boston:

- There are "boat-cars" touring the city at all hours of the day giving Duck Tours. If you make eye contact with the travelers atop this vehicle and shout, "Quack!" They will turn to you and simultaneously reply, "Quack, Quack!"

- A dead body is dragged out of the Charles River way too often. Do not, I repeat, DO NOT, go swimming on an evening of drunken self-exploration. This is a bad idea. I would also avoid contact of said water with both face and other bodily cavities.

- The Boston University Bridge is the only place in the nation where a plane can fly over a car, traveling over a train, going over a boat . . . (or submarine, or Pogo stick, or hovercraft).

- Blue Man Group originated here. Student rush tickets cost only $25 an hour before the show.

- Kurt Vonnegut wrote the majority of his autobiography, *Slapstick*, set just outside of the Boston Public Gardens, where he grew up.

Famous Bostonians:

Samuel Adams
Aerosmith
Louisa May Alcott
The Cars
Ralph Waldo Emerson
Benjamin Franklin
Winslow Homer
Madeleine Kahn

Jack Lemmon
Leonard Nimoy
Edgar Allan Poe
Paul Revere
James Taylor
Kurt Vonnegut
Mark Wahlberg (Marky Mark)
Barbara Walters

→

Local Slang:

Drop your R's . . . they have no business in this city. For way more than you ever wanted to know about Boston slang, visit the "Wicked Good Guide to Boston English" at: *http://www.boston-online.com/glossary.html*.

In the words of Ivy, a character in John Steinbeck's famous novel, *The Grapes of Wrath* (1939):

"'Everybody says words different,' said Ivy. 'Arkansas folks says 'em different, and Oklahomy folks says 'em different. And we seen a lady from Massachusetts, an' she said 'em different of all. Couldn't hardly make out what she was sayin'!'"

Students Speak Out On...
Local Atmosphere

"Boston is cool because there are so many students around, and there are a ton of schools in the area—Boston College, Emerson, Simmons, and Northeastern, to name a few."

Q "Boston is much different from, say, New York, because it is very student oriented and college kid friendly. There are **a lot of places to visit** when you want to be a tourist, such as Quincy Market and the North End (for Italian food)."

Q "**Boston is a college mecca**. There are thousands of colleges in Boston alone, from BC and Emerson, to Berklee College of Music and Northeastern. There's Southie and Back Bay, and Copley is great. The Prudential and Newbury Streets are great for shopping. Chinatown is shady, but it has lots of little shops and great food."

Q "There are so many other colleges around and it **makes for some crazy times** and lots of opportunities to meet people. Boston is definitely a college town. There are so many things to see when you're there. The historic aspect of Boston is fascinating, and it is beautiful all year round."

Q "Boston is the place to be if you're a college student. There are so many things you can do and visit. There are shopping malls, nice restaurants, clubs, 'Broadway' shows, sporting events, museums. Plus, **the city is so rich with history**. You learn a lot about the city in your first year. There are so many other colleges around BU. I'm pretty sure that according to BU, there are about 88 other colleges in the city: Harvard, Boston College, MIT, Babson, Tufts, Brandeis, Northeastern, the University of Massachusetts, and others."

Q "The vibe in Boston is chill if you are in the right area; otherwise, you may find that the people are **a bit on the conservative end**, which is restricting at times. I advise you to search far and wide for the right atmosphere, because it can be hard to find. Don't worry, it's there, and it's waiting for you."

Q "Boston's one of those cities with a lot of different aspects. First off, everybody and their mother goes to school in Boston and attends one of the colleges throughout the city and the outside suburbs. Also, BU has so many people, you meet a new friend, you see a new teacher, a new student, a new RA, and a new jerk all in one day. But like everywhere else in the world, **there are some dangerous places**. There are the usual petty-crime streets where you'll get robbed at knifepoint or even gunpoint. Aside from all the hostility, there are some chill spots to relax and do your thing."

Q "Boston is swarming with college students. The BU atmosphere has a tendency to draw you into its big campus (a.k.a. anywhere along Commonwealth Ave.), so you should **make an effort to explore other parts of the city**— Copley, garment district, Allston, and one of my favorites— Cambridge."

Q "As an elitist, I have had a hard time getting along with the typical university crowd (i.e.: keg parties and the like). The musical scene is pretty diverse, especially for all you hipster, indie-lovers out there. You will see many people hanging around campus grounds during the summer and people racing by during the long winter, striving to beat their frozen feet. Speaking from the perspective of a French student coming from Paris, Boston has a very homey feel, yet, on an entertainment level, it is lacking. Sad to say, **everything in this city closes at two.**"

Q "Boston is a college town. There are a million schools and a million students, **making Boston a very young city**. Stay away from the overpopulated cliché traps like Landsdowne Street. Instead, explore the city and find places like Central Square, Jamaica Plain, and the South End."

The College Prowler Take On...
Local Atmosphere

Boston is a city that is populated by thousands of students, due to the number of universities and colleges (about 60 all together) in the area—something that is also described by most as one of the greatest benefits for BU students. Because there is no reason to be stuck on campus, the best way to have a good experience is to take full advantage of the city.

Because of the overwhelming population of young people in Boston, it is sometimes easy to forget that there are older people and little kids around. Considering this fact, however, the city remains relatively conservative. Everything shuts down at two in the morning (mainly due to Puritan liquor license laws). There are even laws preventing the sale of deodorants on Sunday (this is no longer enforced, but remains in existence).

The College Prowler® Grade on

Local Atmosphere: A+

A high Local Atmosphere grade indicates that the area surrounding campus is safe and scenic. Other factors include nearby attractions, proximity to other schools, and the town's attitude toward students.

Safety & Security

The Lowdown On...
Safety & Security

Number of BU Police:
53

**Number of BU
Security Staff:**
57

**Number of Emergency
Phones:**
50

BU Police Phone:
(617) 353-2121

Safety Services:
BU escort service
Blue-light Phones
Red Phones
Rape hotline
Crisis intervention hotline
Self-defense classes

Health Services:
Medical walk-in clinic
Mental health clinic
Crisis intervention
Rehabilitation services
Counseling center

Health Center Office Hours

Walk-in is available from 9 a.m.-4:30 p.m. every day during the academic year, but is closed on University holidays. The mental health clinic is open from 9 a.m.-5 p.m. during the academic year with 24-hour emergency mental health care at (617) 353-3569 (or 3575). The infirmary is open 24 hours a day during the academic year, with visitation from 1 p.m.-6 p.m. The Crisis Intervention counselors are available 24 hours at (617) 353-2121.

Did You Know?

The office of the Vice President and Dean of Students, located in the GSU (George Sherman Union), distributes the *Lifebook*, which provides information about the details of daily life. This book is a **helpful guide to security procedures and information on campus**.

Students Speak Out On...
Safety & Security

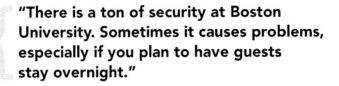

"There is a ton of security at Boston University. Sometimes it causes problems, especially if you plan to have guests stay overnight."

Q "**Boston University is very strict about who can and cannot enter dorms**, and this is one of the biggest issues at BU that people get upset about. There are many dorms on campus, but unless it is a mealtime, you can only get into a dorm other than your own if you are signed in by someone who lives there. After midnight, you can't sign anyone in. So, while this helps keep the dorms safe, it can also get really annoying."

Q "I feel very safe when I'm on campus, and I personally don't feel that security is a problem at BU. Everyone knows where campus security is, and **you see them around all the time**."

Q "Security is a major issue at Boston University. It is very strict, which is good and bad. It's good because **you always feel safe** and you know no one is going to just stroll up and be let into your dorm, but it's bad when it's 12:05 a.m. and you really need to sign someone in but you can't because you can only sign people in until midnight. You cannot just swipe into any of the dorms whenever you want, and the overnight guest policy is very strict—you have to hand in a signed form from yourself and your roommate 24-business hours in advance if it's a same sex visitor, and if it's an opposite sex visitor then you must have a member of the opposite sex on your floor 'host' your visitor. But the RAs usually let your visitor stay with you anyway. It's complicated and very stringent, but no matter what, you will be safe."

Q "Guest policies are constantly being protested as they offer no flexibility and are very restrictive. Seeing as how this is in the middle of Boston, you still have city crime, but the BUPD is pretty much on the ball, and **you rarely hear about anything happening on campus.**"

Q "BU has its own police force, the BUPD. **They are real police officers**, not just security guards (but we have those too in the dorms). The police have real cop cars and guns—the whole bit. There is also a 24-hour number you can call to get free rides on campus if you don't want to have to walk somewhere alone. Security here is very important since it is a major city, and it makes you feel very safe."

Q "There are blue-light phones on every corner at BU, which are phones you can use to call campus security. **I've walked home from the library at 1 a.m.** a couple of times, and I felt completely safe."

Q "The guest policy sucks. **We're treated like immature children at summer camp**. The campus is very safe, though, and I have many times wandered up and down Commonwealth Avenue early in the morning without any problems."

Q "The security is tip-top considering that I have never had any problems. At times, **I have been, I must say, on my guard walking down a dark alley past bedtime**. But have no fear! The BU police are here, and they will know just what to say when you are in distress."

Q "Safety and security is really good considering we're in the middle of Boston. The campus stretches for a couple miles. Don't worry, though, because the subway (known as the T) goes right down the middle of the street. There really isn't a real problem with it, but **the BU police do offer an escort service** if you feel you ever need one. All you have to do is call them up, and an officer will go with you to make you feel safer."

Q "**Security is structured completely backwards**. They spend so much time making sure security is as tight as possible in the freshmen dorms that the rest of the University seems to be completely overlooked. I don't think BU police patrol the streets where the majority of BU students live."

Q "Security is pretty good overall. There are Boston cops and BU cops all over, even when you don't want them there; plus almost every dorm has a security guard on duty 24/7. Flip side, though, is **security often just gets in the way and causes trouble for students**. I mean, we're college students, we're almost adults, and we can protect ourselves for the most part, so we don't need a big brother watching us constantly. Yeah, you'll feel safe, but once in a while, you stumble in drunk without your ID card, and you can't get into the building. Sometimes, due to the actions of the guards, you may even find yourself at the police station or the emergency room. But at least you are safe, I guess."

Q "Since there really is no BU 'campus,' you're pretty much just getting around in the city. If you're from a big city, then Boston seems pretty safe. **There are blue phones everywhere**. As far as dorm safety, it's pretty much over-the-top. You definitely don't have to worry about strange bums coming into the dorms, but you also might have a big problem trying to get someone you met at the bar to stay with you overnight. Better make other plans, hot stuff."

The College Prowler Take On...
Safety & Security

There is no question, students feel safe on campus. Most people even report feeling perfectly comfortable roaming the area alone at night. The overwhelming presence of campus security, however, does put a significant strain on student life in the dorms. Avoiding the larger on-campus housing options is universally suggested to decrease problems with the stringent guest policies and curfews adhered to at BU. Bay State Road and South Campus housing do not have security guards at the entrance, thereby allowing for more freedom.

To be honest, it is not that difficult to avoid interaction with campus security. The University is littered with blue-light phones, there is a 24-hour crisis hotline, and there's an escort service for late-night traveling (which, by the way, is the best way to get from one end of campus to the other for free). I have always felt safe walking around campus at all hours—there are almost always people out and about—even after the rest of the city shuts down. My favorite time of day is 5 a.m. because there are no cars on the road, and you can dance in the streets.

B+

The College Prowler® Grade on
Safety & Security: B+

A high grade in Safety & Security means that students generally feel safe, campus police are visible, blue-light phones and escort services are readily available, and safety precautions are not overly necessary.

Computers

The Lowdown On...
Computers

High-Speed Network?
Yes, Boston University Campus Network (supporting up to 100 million bits per second)

Number of Labs:
37

Operating Systems:
PC, MAC, Linux and UNIX

Wireless Network?
Yes, Mugar Memorial Library (basement and floors 1-3), the Science and Engineering Library, the Pappas Law Library (and many other parts of the School of Law), the Photonics Research Center (floors 1-5), the West Campus Dining Facility, the School of Management (floors 1-3), the public areas of floors 1, 2, 3, and 5 of the George Sherman Union, including the Food Court, and the Faculty & Staff Dining Room

Discounted Software

University Computers sells hardware, software, supplies, and accessories. The service department offers repair and upgrade services. You can find literally hundreds of software programs priced at major educational discounts.

24-Hour Labs

ACS (UNIX cluster and central e-mail server) Help Desk, Campus Network, and Information Technology Computer Lab (all at 111 Cummington St.).

Charge to Print?

Each student receives up to 500 free pages per semester at the main computer lab on Cummington St. and most others on campus. At some of the smaller labs (CAS), the fee is 10 cents per page. You can use your BU ID card to print at a limited number of local photocopying businesses in the immediate area.

Did You Know?

If you don't log out after a session on any of the campus computers, you are at risk. Your personal user name and password are necessary to gain access to your records. If you do not sign out of your session, it is possible for another individual to acquire this personal information about your academic status. Some students are definitely guilty of printing long term papers on another careless student's open account. The moral of the story? Don't forget to log out.

A Note About the Internet:

BU is a member of Internet2 (NoX)—a national organization which operates a high-performance communications exchange. This allows the University to be connected to the Internet2 network, thereby providing us with very high-speed access to hundreds of other institutions connected to similarly advanced networks around the world.

Students Speak Out On...
Computers

"Definitely bring your own computer. There are computer labs in most dorms, and there's a computer center, but you'll absolutely want to have your own."

Q "One of the really nice things about college is the fast Internet connections, so you can download every song you ever wanted. The computer network is really fast, and it's cool because **people put stuff onto the network that is shared by everybody like music, and movies**. I don't know what your major is, but if you can possibly get a computer to bring to school, you should, even if it's just a really basic one. You'll probably be doing a lot of typing throughout the year, and having Internet access is really important for a lot of classes. There are computer labs near every dorm, if not in them, so if you don't have a computer don't freak out. But I would definitely recommend one, even if it's only for the purpose of using Instant Messenger."

Q "**The network at BU is great**, and every room has an Ethernet set up for each person (the Ethernet is amazing). I would definitely bring your own computer, just for convenience, but the computer lab in my dorm (Rich Hall) was never crowded."

Q "Computer labs are pretty good, but they're **usually pretty crowded**. When it comes time to write papers, midterms and finals, it's crazy in the labs. Your own computer is a really good idea. You just need to buy an Ethernet card because there is a connection in just about every part of campus. It's well worth it."

Q "I brought my own computer, and I'm so glad that I did. It is way more convenient to have one in your room than to have to go to the lab. **The lab is only crowded at specific times**."

Q "Bring your own computer. We have a T3 Internet connection, so **you can download hundreds of megs of data in a few minutes**. I never needed to use the computer labs much, but they usually aren't full."

Q "There's always a computer to be used. My laptop broke, and I was too lazy to fix it for five months, but I still found a computer to use any time I needed one. There are multiple computer labs, and all your friends will have them, too. Nevertheless, **a personal computer is always preferable, but again, you don't need one**. On the other hand, if you have your own, you'll usually have a fast connection to download music, games, programs, notes, homework—whatever you need at a pretty good speed."

Q "**The computer network is addictive**. That was definitely the only thing I was craving when I moved off campus. There are always tons of people in the main computer lab, and it's most crowded around lunchtime. But besides the computer in your dorm (if you choose to bring one, which you definitely should), there are other places that you can go to get onto the network."

Q "If you can afford it, get a computer. If not, there are plenty of facilities on campus, at a variety of locations, that will be able to accommodate your Internet needs. Prepare yourself for **20- to 40-minute waits when printing** at the main computer lab on Cummington Street. Here is a tip: go the printing center in Warren Towers during daytime hours. All campus facilities, in the spirit of socialism, have high-speed Internet."

Q "**Computer labs are usually spacious**, except around exam time. Having a PC, however, saves you from emergency situations, and it is a convenient resource for just about everything."

Q "Bring your own computer. Not only that, but **bring your own printer**, because you may not be able to print out a paper at the last minute in the computer labs, and God knows what is going to happen. The computer lab is nice. Not many people know about my secret spot—the Warren Towers computer lab. Side-note: if you are doing research, and you have to find a lot of stuff, print in the IT, because you can print up to 500 pages there, and you can use the resources that BU provides you, without giving them more of your hard-earned money."

Q "**Instant Messaging is life**—if you don't have it, get it. IM is always on, and you don't even need a campus phone if you have a computer because everyone is online all the time. Things change a little after freshman year because not everyone can afford a DSL connection once they venture off campus, but for the most part, particularly freshman year, IM will be your doorway to social betterment and partying pleasures."

The College Prowler Take On...
Computers

If you have the means to do so, bringing your own computer will save you a lot of hassle. The University provides Ethernet in all of the dorms, and it is pretty cheap to set up high-speed Internet even off campus. Almost all the facilities on campus are equipped with Internet connections, so a laptop is probably your best bet. If you do need to use campus computers, there are always people to help out, and printing is free at most locations. Unfortunately, the only major 24-hour computer lab tends to get really crowded, and if you're in a hurry, it can be frustrating—so leave yourself plenty of time.

I literally could not have survived school without my laptop. If you do bring your own computer, it will quickly become your most important asset. Not only is it a good tool for your academics, but it also allows you to stay in constant contact with friends from home and at school. You can talk to your mom, chat with your friend down the hall, plan your trip to Vegas for spring break, play Tetris, download Simpsons episodes, write your thesis, check the weather, find a good show to check out on the weekend, and watch porn, all at the same time. Beat that. Word of advice: back up everything. I had a computer die on me, and all of my work, my music, my life, was suddenly taken out of existence. Computers get stolen, lost, broken, and worn down, so be prepared.

B+

The College Prowler® Grade on

Computers: B+

A high grade in Computers designates that computer labs are available, the computer network is easily accessible, and the campus' computing technology is up-to-date.

Facilities

The Lowdown On...
Facilities

Student Center:
The George Sherman Union
(GSU)

Athletic Centers:
The Case Athletic Center

Indoor tennis and track Center

Agganis Ice Hockey Arena

Student Village Fitness and
Recreation Center

Dance Theater

Libraries:
23, (2.3 million volumes,
29,389 periodicals, 4.1 million
microfilm units)

Popular Places to Chill:
The BU Beach

The GSU

The West Campus area/
Nickerson Field

Marsh Chapel Plaza

Espresso Royale Café

The Charles River Esplanade

Campus Size:
133 acres

➔

What Is There to Do on Campus?

There is so much to do on campus that your best bet for up-to-date events and information is to check the BU Student Union Web site at *http://www.bu.edu/union*.

Movie Theater on Campus?

The Nickelodeon (Nick), which was torn down in 2004, and has been replaced by the Life Sciences and Engineering building located on Cummington Street. Nick was used to hold classes, as well as operating as a fully-functioning theater. Kevin Spacey was a guest there at a premier of "American Beauty" held a few years back. While there is currently no other theater on campus, the rumor is the Nick will be reopened within the next few years.

Bar on Campus?

Yes, the notorious BU Pub is the only bar located on campus that is officially affiliated with the University. There are several other bars located on the Commonwealth stretch, including T's Pub, the Paradise Lounge, and several sports bars.

Coffeehouse on Campus?

Yes, while there are countless coffeehouses in the area, the most popular café that attracts BU students (aside from the Starbucks located in a variety of the buildings on campus) is Espresso Royale Café, or lovingly known as the ERC. This is a really chill place to study or socialize right in the middle of BU.

Students Speak Out On...

Facilities

"The George Sherman Union is a big hangout and study center."

Q "Right now, BU is reconstructing a lot of buildings. They have recently finished building all new athletic facilities which are really, really nice. There are a lot of gyms to work out at or play basketball in, and they have lots of fitness classes that you can take. There are some nice computer labs around, too, with a lot of computers. The student union is cool. Its main feature is the food court. The **classrooms range from being really, really nice to kind of crappy**."

Q "**Some buildings are old and crappy, but others are new and state-of-the-art**. There's a wide variety. Overall, the buildings are up-to-date on technology, and they are going through a lot of renovations."

Q "Certain colleges have older buildings than others. In the sports center, we have a swimming pool, ice rink, and a bunch of different courts in just one building. Our student center is pretty much just the George Sherman Union (the food court) or lounges in your individual dorms. If you're looking for a school with a strong sense of community, then you don't want this place. We're **spread throughout the city**, all within walking distance, but you don't get that community sense."

Q "All the computer labs have Dell desktops, and they got a bunch of new ones recently. **The Student Center (GSU) is always filled with students**, and it's a nice place to eat dinner, watch a sports game, and get together with your friends."

Q "Everything on BU's campus is very nice. It's either new, or it's **old, but architecturally beautiful**. I would say that Commonwealth Avenue is the main road on campus, and since it is a city campus, it's very concrete-looking, with no big fields of green grass like other places."

Q "For the most part, all the facilities at BU are **definitely high-quality**. They have just about everything. The computer center's all right, except that there are not enough computers down there. But apparently, there is more than one lab, so they say. Anyway, the student union is pretty phat. They have a smoking lounge, or rather they had a smoking lounge. But I guess it's still nice. There is some good food and a lot of seating. Some people spend their entire year doing work there, but it's still not the best student union."

Q "Well, I wasn't one to exercise, but if you want a nice gym to work out in, Case Gym is the one to go to. **It gets really crowded** around and after dinnertime, and you might have to fight people off for a turn on the elliptical machine. The GSU was one of my favorite places to be. I spent hours of my life in the smoking lounge . . . but because of that new smoking law, it doesn't exist for your smoking 'n studying pleasure (sigh)."

Q "The gym is decent. There is also **a really good student union**. There is a lot of fast food that you can burn off at the decent gym. I never do, but you could."

Q "**The facilities are well kept**. The student union is mostly commercial, as exemplified by the food and the expensive booths selling gifts, jewelry, clothes, CDs, movies, and video games that litter the lobby; but then again, activities and organizations are not really BU's forte."

Q "**The work-out room kind of sucks**; I highly advise you to get a membership at Wellbridge Fitness Club instead, if you have the money. They have a hot tub and a pool."

The College Prowler Take On...
Facilities

Recently, the administration has put a lot of money and effort into the improvement of the student facilities on campus. While students have noticed the improvements, no one seemed to be especially moved by the change. In comparison with other schools in the area, the University certainly has a large amount of money to play with, and most buildings are up-to-date and well-equipped for student needs.

Many of the facilities are currently being remodeled and updated, including the new athletic center, student dorms, and parking facilities. Depending on the particular colleges—which tend to receive different amounts of funding—some buildings are in better condition than others. All of the dining halls, especially in the West Campus and the Student Village, have just been renovated in the past few years. Unfortunately, all of these changes also imply that a lot of construction is constantly taking place around campus (which is a nice atmosphere, if you are into that whole industrial look). Currently, most of the work is located around the new senior dorms, which look more like hotels—a definite hot-spot for on campus living and an incentive to keep students on BU grounds.

B+

The College Prowler® Grade on

Facilities: B+

A high Facilities grade indicates that the campus is aesthetically pleasing and well-maintained; facilities are state-of-the-art, and libraries are exceptional. Other determining factors include the quality of both athletic and student centers and an abundance of things to do on campus.

Campus Dining

The Lowdown On...
Campus Dining

Freshman Meal Plan Requirement?

Yes

Meal Plan Average Cost:

$3,358

Places to Grab a Bite with Your Meal Plan:

Bread Winners

Food: Sandwiches, soups, salads, snacks

Location: School of Management: 595 Commonwealth Avenue, 2nd floor

Favorite Dish: Cream of broccoli soup

Hours: Monday–Thursday 7:30 a.m.–6 p.m., Friday 7:30 a.m.–2:30 p.m.

➜

Café 575

Food: Gourmet coffee, fruit smoothies, sandwiches, and pastries

Location: 575 Commonwealth Ave.

Favorite Dish: piña colada smoothie

Hours: Daily 7 a.m.–1 a.m.

Domino's Pizza

Food: Pizza, wings, cinnamon sticks

Location: 1314 Boylston St.

Favorite Dish: pineapple pizza with blue cheese dressing on the side

Hours: Monday–Thursday 11 a.m.–2 a.m., Friday–Sunday 11 a.m.–3 a.m.

Ferretti's

Food: Sandwiches, scones, muffins, bagels, juice, coffees, salads, fruit

Location: 700 Commonwealth Ave.

Favorite Dish: Herbed Foccaccia (focaccia with basil, fresh mozzarella, and tomato)

Hours: Monday–Thursday 7:30 a.m.–8 p.m., Friday 7:30 a.m.–5 p.m., Saturday–Sunday and holidays 10 a.m.–6 p.m.

Hillel Kosher Dining Room

Food: Kosher

Location: 233 Bay State Rd.

Favorite Dish: holiday specials

Hours: Monday–Friday 11:30 a.m.–2 p.m. Saturday 12 p.m.–2 p.m.. Dinner Hours: Monday–Thursday 5 p.m.–7 p.m., Friday–Saturday 7 p.m.–8 p.m., (*These times may vary. Friday dinner and Saturday lunch begin immediately following services).

Late Night Café

Food: Fried foods, stir fry, quesadillas, salads, fruit, chips, cookies, giant rice krispy treats

Location: Myles Standish Hall, The Towers, and Shelton Hall, Warren Towers, West Campus

Favorite Dish: Stir fry

Hours: Monday–Thursday 8:30 p.m.–12 a.m., Friday–Sunday 8:30 p.m.–12 a.m.

Myles Standish Dining Hall

Food: Breakfast, lunch, and dinner are served cafeteria-style

Location: 610 Beacon St.

Favorite Dish: Salad bar

Hours: Monday–Thursday 7 a.m.–8 p.m., Friday 7 a.m.–7 p.m., Saturday 9 a.m.–7 p.m., Sunday 10:30 a.m.–8 p.m.

Science Fare

Food: Sandwiches

Location: 590 Commonwealth Ave., Basement

Favorite Dish: Cheese sandwich

Hours: Monday–Thursday 8 a.m.–4 p.m., Friday 8 a.m.–3 p.m.

Shelton Hall Dining

Food: Breakfast, lunch, and dinner are served cafeteria-style

Location: 91 Bay State Road

Favorite Dish: Anything from the grill

Hours: Monday–Thursday 7 a.m.–8 p.m., Friday 7 a.m.–7 p.m., Saturday 9 a.m.–7 p.m., Sunday 10:30 a.m.–8 p.m.

The Towers

Food: Breakfast, lunch, and dinner are served cafeteria-style

Location: 140 Bay State Rd.

Favorite Dish: Potato bar

Hours: Monday–Thursday 7 a.m.–8 p.m., Friday 7 a.m.–7 p.m., Saturday 9 a.m.–7 p.m., Sunday 10:30 a.m.–8 p.m.

Union Court

Food: Aesops Bagels, Amalfi Oven, Burger King, Caprito Burritos, Copper Kettle, Cranberry Farms, D'Angelo Sandwich Shops, Fruit Market, Loose Leafs, Jamba Juice, Sushi

Location: The George Sherman Union—775 Commonwealth Ave.

Favorite Dish: Mango-a-go-go (Jamba Juice)

Hours: Times vary for each individual restaurant in the food court. For a quick overview of schedules, check *http://www.bu.edu/dining* and look under "retail," and then click on the "Union Court" option.

Warren Towers Dining Hall

Food: Breakfast, lunch, and dinner are served cafeteria-style

Location: 700 Commonwealth Avenue

Favorite Dish: Burrito bar

Hours: Monday–Thursday 7 a.m.–8 p.m., Friday 7 a.m.–7 p.m., Saturday 9 a.m.–7 p.m., Sunday 10:30 a.m.–8 p.m.

Off-Campus Places to Use Your Meal Plan:

Domino's Pizza accepts BU Dining Points and Convenience Points. Call (617) 254-4800.

24-Hour On-Campus Eating?

Just the Store 24s along Commonwealth Avenue and a couple Dunkin Donuts off campus.

Did You Know?

Dining Services offers a variety of special events throughout the year, including a Visiting Chef Series; lobster, shrimp scampi, and prime rib dinners; fondue festival; North End Dessert tour; and holiday meals.

FYI: At the end of the academic year, the **dining plans refund 100% on unused Convenience Points**, 50% on unused Dining Points, and none on unused meals.

Student Favorites

The GSU accepts BU dining points and convenience points at their food court, which is comprised of several independently-operating eateries, including Burger King, Aesop's Bagels, Jamba Juice, Starbucks, Copper Kettle (soup), Burrito Grande, and D'Angelo's Subs. There is also a salad bar, fruit bar, yogurt, a full-service sushi bar, and snacks. Ferretti's is another popular place for on-campus eating. They have really good sandwiches that are fashioned similarly to Au Bon Pan, bagels, gourmet coffee, fruit salad, scones, and muffins.

Students Speak Out On...
Campus Dining

> "The food, for the most part, is pretty good. There are a lot of dining halls around campus, and each one is slightly different, which is good."

Q "If you're a picky eater, there's always pasta, sandwiches or salad to eat. At the student union, they also have a food court where you can use your dining points to buy Burger King, Ben & Jerry's, D'Angelo's, and pizza, among other things. **The food does get repetitive**, but the good thing about being in Boston is that there are tons of places to eat if you want to go out for dinner (that are all in walking distance)."

Q "The food is pretty good, but I'd have to say that **Warren Dining Hall has the best food on campus**. Best bets for take out: Wing It and Angora Cafè."

Q "**The food is really good**. It does, however, get repetitive in the dining halls, and that's when the student union comes in handy. The University gives you a certain amount of dining points that you use there. Cash is a thing of the past. The student union has Burger King, D'angelo's (subs), Late Nite Cafè, Copper Kettle, plus more."

Q "Dorm food is so-so. It tastes good at first, then it gets old fast! I think this is typical of all schools, though. **I like our meal plan**, where you use a 'meal' and then it's all-you-can-eat."

Q "BU's dining halls are, by far, some of the best in the country. My favorite dining hall is in the Towers, which is a mostly-freshman dorm. If you have the choice, I definitely recommend living there. Besides the dining halls, there are tons of places around campus with all different types of cuisine. **My favorite is Amalfi Oven**. It's got calzones, pizza, and it's cheap!"

Q "Food isn't really all that bad. Of course it's going to be somewhat bad; it's dorm food. However, they make a **good effort to meet the dietary needs of everyone**, and the food is decent because they have to feed wealthy international students. My preference is definitely West Campus. The dining hall there is set up like a restaurant more than a cafeteria. The smaller dorms are also nice, like Shelton and Myles. Warren really isn't that bad, and it's open until 12 a.m. for late-night eating, so if you live in Warren (most freshmen do) it's really not as bad as it's made out to be."

Q "West Campus recently renovated their dining hall; it has a restaurant atmosphere, and the food is awesome. Food at Warren Towers is okay, and **the dining hall is very convenient** since it's in the middle of the campus."

Q "On-campus food is actually pretty good. When they have **annual lobster nights**, the line is out the door."

Q "While you'll hear all the students complain, the food is actually very good compared to all the other universities and colleges around. Just about **every dorm has its own dining hall** where you can get breakfast, lunch and dinner. We also have a central food court (George Sherman Union) where you can find Burger King, D'Angelo's and various other fast food restaurants that accept both dining points and cash."

Q "All of the big dining halls have pretty good food. Also, every night there is the 'Late-Night Café,' which is in the dining hall, and then, instead of the usual buffet, you pay for what you eat. They also serve late-night snacks like chips, soda, fruit smoothies, french fries, chicken fingers—you get the deal. **Every dining hall is a little different**. Some have a more modern style, with little booths and smaller tables, and others have the traditional big round tables for like 8-10 people. You just have to go to all of them and decide what you like best, but that is usually determined by where you live on campus."

Q "The Warren dining hall is good, and West Campus recently built a fancy dining hall. The food is decent. Also, the GSU (student union) provides more variety: Burger King, pizza, D'Angelo's, Pasta Works, Jamba Juice, a soup bar, and a really good salad bar. They also have sushi, sandwiches, fresh fruit, Starbucks, and a bagel place. **You won't go hungry**."

Q "Boston University has a **duality to its food selection**. On the one side, you have got some great food at West Campus and Myles. It's a large selection that ranges from everything to everything else. But if you're stuck in Warren Towers, then you have the lower end of the food. You've got the McDonald's burger compared to the filet mignon of West Campus."

Q "I'm sorry, but BU food is **stupendous compared to some of the crap I've eaten** at other universities when visiting friends. They recently redid the West Campus dining hall, so you feel pretty superstar when you walk into the futuristic dining area. Plus, you must try the burrito; I'm like Ozzy Osbourne—I love the burrito. I live for the burrito. Almost every dorm has a dining hall, so it's pretty convenient. Warren Towers has the largest selection, but the quality is not that great."

The College Prowler Take On...
Campus Dining

While it is not uncommon to hear complaints about the food, all students will agree that BU is pretty hooked-up in that department. There is a huge variety and tons of places to use your meal plan around campus. The big suggestions for getting your money's worth are to check out the specialty nights and the smaller eateries on campus. Remember, the meals are not refundable, but most meal plans provide many more than you need. If you do the math, each meal costs about nine dollars, so eat up. Even if you just stop by for an ice cream, you may as well use the meals that you are paying for anyway.

The food at BU was rated second in the country, so I guess it's good. It is good. The presentation is very well done, too, so even if it doesn't taste right, it looks like it should. After four years though, I don't care how incredible the food is . . . it is all the same to me.

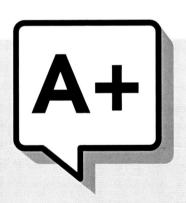

The College Prowler® Grade on

Campus Dining: A+

Our grade on Campus Dining addresses the quality of both school-owned dining halls and independent on-campus restaurants as well as the price, availability, and variety of food.

Off-Campus Dining

The Lowdown On...
Off-Campus Dining

Restaurant Prowler:
Popular Places to Eat!

Angora Café
Food: Healthy, wraps, frozen yogurt, pizza
1024 Commonwealth Avenue
(617) 232-1757
Cool Features: Outdoor seating, big screen TV, comfortable couches
Price: $2–$10
Hours: Monday–Saturday 8 a.m.–11:30 a.m., Sunday 9 a.m.–11:30 a.m.

Anna's Taqueria
Food: Mexican
1412 Beacon Street
(617) 739-7300
Cool Features: Fast service
Price: $5–$10
Hours: Daily 10 a.m.–11 p.m.

Buddha's Delight
Food: Vegetarian Asian
404 Harvard Avenue
(617) 739-8830
Cool Features: Free tea
Price: $5–$15
Hours: Monday–Thursday, Friday–Saturday 11 a.m.–10:30 p.m., Sunday 11 a.m.–9:30 p.m.

Cookin' Cafe
Food: Breakfast
1096 Commonwealth Avenue
(617) 566-4144
Cool Features: Fabulous omlettes
Price: $5–$15
Hours: Daily 8 a.m.–12 a.m.

Maggiano's Little Italy
Food: Italian
4 Columbus Avenue
(617) 542-3456
Cool Features: Traditional-style Italian food
Price: $10-$30
Hours: Monday–Thursday
11:30 a.m.–2:30 p.m.,
5 p.m.–10 p.m.,
Friday 10:30 a.m.–2:30 p.m.,
5 p.m.–10 p.m., Saturday
11:30 a.m.–3 p.m., 4 p.m.–
10:30 p.m., Sunday
11:30 a.m.–10 p.m.

Nud Pob Thai Cuisine
Food: Thai
708 Commonwealth Avenue
(617) 536-8676
Cool Features: Located right in central campus
Price: $5–$15
Hours: Monday–Friday
11:30 a.m.–11 p.m., Saturday–
Sunday 12 p.m.–10:30 p.m.

P.F. Chang's
Food: Pan-Asian
8 Park Place
(617) 573-0821
Cool Features: Lots of different mixed drinks
Price: $10–$20
Hours: Monday–Wednesday,
Sunday 11:30 a.m.–11 p.m.,
Thursday–Saturday
11:30 a.m.–12 a.m.

Steve's Kitchen
Food: Diner food
120 Harvard Avenue
(617) 254-9457
Cool Features: Diner atmosphere, breakfast is served all day
Price: $5–$15
Hours: Monday–Saturday
6 p.m.–6 p.m., Sunday 6 a.m.–
6 p.m.

T-Anthony's
Food: Italian/pizza
1016 Commonwealth Avenue
(617) 734-7708
Cool Features: BU paraphernalia covers the walls, always packed with students
Price: $2–$10
Hours: Monday–Saturday
7 a.m.–2 a.m., Sunday 8 a.m.–
1 a.m.

The Upper Crust

Food: Pizza

20 Charles Street

(617) 723-9600

Cool Features: Great pizza and terrific atmosphere (three big-screen HDTVs)

Price: $5–$20

Hours: Sunday–Wednesday 11:30 a.m.–10 p.m., Thursday–Saturday 11:30 a.m.–10:30 p.m.

Wing it

Food: Wings

1153 Commonwealth Avenue

(617) 783-2473

Cool Features: Conveniently located between BU and BC

Price: $7–$20

Hours: Monday–Thursday 4 p.m.–12 a.m., Friday–Saturday 12 p.m.–2 a.m., Sunday 12 p.m.–12 a.m.

Best Pizza:
The Upper Crust

Best Chinese:
P.F. Chang's

Best Breakfast:
Cookin' Café

Best Wings:
Wing It

Best Healthy:
Angora's Cafe

Best Place to Take Your Parents:
Any of the restaurants in the North End (Maggiano's is a common favorite)

Closest Grocery Store:
Shaw's Supermarket
1065 Commonwealth Avenue, Brighton
(617) 783-5878

Did You Know?

Late-Night Snacking

For **late night munchies**, hit up a Store 24 or a Dunkin' Donuts. Drew and Greg's late-night cookies delivers hot, freshly baked cookies to your door, but only until midnight (1-866-EAT-LATE).

BU offers **Late-Night Cafés** around campus at all of the traditional dining halls. Late-Night usually offers quesadillas, stir-fry, fried food, salad, fruit, chips, cookies, beverages, coffee, and the ever-popular giant rice crispy treats.

24-Hour Eating

Boston is definitely lacking in the 24-hour department. There is only one 24-hour diner open in Boston, and it is way downtown.

Fun Facts

Try Chinatown for a night out . . . not only is it home to the best Chinese food in Boston, but most restaurants serve alcohol without requesting identification. This is a good place for an underage outing. Ask for a Scorpion Bowl.

Don't Forget

Domino's Pizza delivers until 3 a.m., and it takes BU Dining Points. Ask for free cinnamon sticks with any large pizza.

Student Favorites

T-Anthony's is like 90210's Peach Pit. It is practically encrusted with BU paraphernalia and students, and is located at the central location in West Campus. T's serves pizza, subs, and pretty decent Italian food. They also have really good smoothies and breakfast foods. If the typical BU crowd makes you lose your appetite, this is not the place to be.

Students Speak Out On...
Off-Campus Dining

"Off-campus, Boston offers plenty of restaurants throughout the city. The possibilities are truly endless, so it depends on what kind of food you want. T-Anthony's is great to start out with; it is Italian food with huge portions."

Q "The North End is a must for Italian food. Dolce Vita is my favorite because the owner sings at night. On Commonwealth Avenue, which is BU's home, Brown Sugar and Siam Cuisine have great Thai food. There is always a wealth of pizza and subs shops around campus, as well."

Q "There are a lot of good restaurants. There are chain restaurants like Uno's, California Pizza Kitchen, Chili's, and TGI Friday's nearby; and then there are a lot of other good places, too."

Q "The Elephant Walk is a really good, kind of pricey French and Cambodian place. It sounds weird, but it's really good. The restaurants on Newbury Street (the popular shopping/eating street) are all pretty good and semi-pricey. The North End is all Italian food; it's really good and kind of pricey. California Pizza Kitchen is good and Legal Sea Foods is good for seafood, which is very popular in the New England area."

Q "You can find lots of stuff on Commonwealth Avenue where BU is situated. Clio is one of the hot spots, and so is the Thai House. If you want to go off Commonwealth Avenue, then you can hop the Green Line to Newbury Street, or the Prudential."

Q "**I love Brown Sugar**; it's a Thai restaurant on Commonwealth Avenue. Anna's is also a really great Mexican spot, but nothing beats downtown. Quincy Market is a great place to shop and eat; it has a million different kinds of foods all in a 'mall-like' food court. For nicer dining, there is great stuff up and down Newbury Street (it's very Euro and full of designer shops). And, of course, the staple of college life—pizza. I really don't recommend any particular pizza place, but for a cheap slice of pizza, Sicilia's and Alexander's are decent."

Q "Boston restaurants are fabulous, especially if you like seafood. The North End has really good Italian food. Maggiano's Little Italy downtown is my new favorite restaurant. Newbury Street has a lot of good little cafes and stuff. **The Pour House on Boylston Street is good**, as well as Vinny T's."

Q "Outside of BU jurisdiction, there are some real good restaurants, real good. There is La Mamas, University Grill, and Domino's Pizza on BU dining points, which is by far the single greatest thing BU has ever done. Thank you BU, I loved the free pizza. Also there are a lot of other restaurants around, way too many to name. **You can essentially find any type of food you want**, from Chinese to Indian, to Spanish, to Colombian, to American to Turkish, and even Syrian."

Q "Boston has a lot of good restaurants. Ginza for Japanese, Angora's for wraps, and really good fro-yo. If you go to BU, then you eat pizza at T's, Rangoli's for Indian, **Sunset Grill for like 5 million beers on tap**, Cheesecake Factory in the Copley Mall, P.F. Chang's for really good Chinese, The Middle East for excellent (guess) Middle Eastern food, and it's also a venue and they usually have some pretty good shows for cheap there."

Q "Boston has a good selection of restaurants; I should know, I eat out all the time. **If you like the vegetarian ordeal, hit up Buddha's Delight**, either in Brookline or in Chinatown. If not, Grasshopper isn't bad either. If you are down for the deli, this city isn't going to satisfy your needs, unless you go to Rubin's or Zaftigs, which are both on Harvard Avenue in Brookline. For Italian, you can always be sure to get a good meal in a little trattoria in the North End. I always liked to eat at the Pour House on Boylston Street because it is really cheap and has a good atmosphere. Near campus, try An Tua Nua; there is good music, good food and drinks, good prices, and good people. If you are just looking for a slice of pizza, before all of you New Yorkers complain that your pizza is better, check out the Upper Crust. Alright, that is quite enough of the gastronomical tour, as I could go on for hours."

Q "Thai food is good. There is also a **yummy frozen yogurt place called Angora's Café in West Campus** that was always a nightly treat. That Chinese place next door, Quan's Kitchen, has a General Tso's chicken that is delish."

Q "I really enjoyed the **new Thai and Indian restaurants in the Allston area**. There were not as many Italian restaurants, unless you go to the North End. And realistically, how many times are you going to go to the North End? Okay, find some friends with money who are willing to make some expenditure for good food. Otherwise, you will be ordering take-out, which is not as fun, nor as tasty, and you will wind up spending money anyway. If you have no friends, your best bet is to go to the supermarket."

The College Prowler Take On...
Off-Campus Dining

Students all have a suggestion for just about every type of cuisine you could ask for. There are virtually no complaints regarding the food in Boston. Restaurants off campus vary as widely as the city—offering pretty much everything. Going out to eat definitely seems to be a popular activity, and the prices tend to be pretty reasonable, especially around campus.

Clustered around the University, especially in the Allston/Brighton area, where many students live, there are tons of really cheap options with really good food such as Indian, vegetarian, Mexican, Brazilian, Italian, Chinese, Thai, and Vietnamese. Check out Chinatown and the North End for the best food in the city.

The College Prowler® Grade on

Off-Campus
Dining: A

A high Off-Campus Dining grade implies that off-campus restaurants are affordable, accessible, and worth visiting. Other factors include the variety of cuisine and the availability of alternative options (vegetarian, vegan, Kosher, etc.).

Campus Housing

The Lowdown On...
Campus Housing

Room Types:

Double, triple, and quad room (standard minimum fee)

Multiple-occupancy room in suite

Suite in 1019 Commonwealth Avenue and Shelton Hall

Single without private bath

Single with private bath

Apartment with two or more students

Single room in an apartment

Apartment with one student

Best Dorms:

Bay State brownstones, The Student Village, West Campus

Worst Dorms:

Warren Towers, The Towers

Number of Dormitory Residents:

10,776

Undergrads Living on Campus:

74%

→

Dormitory Residences:

575 Commonwealth Ave.

Floors: 8

Number of Occupants: 450

Bathrooms: Private baths

Coed: Yes

Room Types: Triple-occupancy, with doubles and singles on the top floor

Special Features: Air-conditioning, lofted furniture, blackout curtains, study lounge on top floor with a view of the Charles River, 24-hour study lounge, Café 575, vending machines, laundry, mail room, recycling

Residents: Under- and upperclassmen

Warren Towers Complex

(Fairfield, Marshall, and Shields)

700 Commonwealth Ave.

Floors: 18

Number of Occupants: 1,755

Bathrooms: 2 common baths per floor

Coed: Yes, single-sex floors are available

Room Types: 18 doubles, one triple, and four singles per floor

Special Features: cinema room, dining hall, music practice room, game room, roof access, computer lab with printing, and the ground level contains a Fleet Bank, Ferretti's Bagel Shop, Copy Center, and a Campus Convenience

Residents: Underclassmen

Student Village

10 Buick St.

Number of Occupants: 817

Bathrooms: One in each suite

Coed: Yes

Room Types: 4-bedroom apartments, 2-bedroom apartments, all single rooms

Special Features: Central air, view of the river, fully furnished, mail room, laundry, fitness room, computer lab, study rooms, music practice rooms, cafe, convenience store

Residents: Only Upperclassman allowed

1019 Commonwealth Ave.

Floors: 6

Number of Occupants: 275

Bathrooms: Each suite has its own bathroom

Coed: Yes

Room Types: Three doubles forming a six-person suite with a common room

Special Features: Large common study room, TV lines in each room, close to facilities at Case Athletic Center, laundry

Residents: Upperclassmen

Danielsen Hall

512 Beacon St.

Floors: 8

Number of Occupants: approximately 600

Bathrooms: Some rooms have private baths

Coed: Yes

Room Types: Single-, double-, and triple-occupancy suites.

Special Features: Formal living room, TV lounge with common kitchen facility, study rooms, laundry room, mail room, pool tables, Ping Pong tables, access to cable television, indoor bike rack, vending machines, and a shuttle bus

Residents: Under- and upperclassmen

Myles Standish Hall

610 Beacon St.

Floors: 8

Number of Occupants: 672

Bathrooms: Three to six residents share a common bath per suite

Coed: Yes

Room Types: Suites with three to six residents

Special Features: Dining hall, mail room, fitness room, game room, computer lab, music room, and laundry room

Residents: Under- and upperclassmen

Myles Annex

632 Beacon St. (accessed from the 2nd Floor at Myles Standish Hall)

Floors: 3

Number of Occupants: 93

Bathrooms: Communal per floor

Coed: Yes

Room Types: Double-, triple-occupancy

Special Features: Mail room, dining room, laundry, fitness room, and computer room

Residents: Upperclassmen

Shelton Hall

91 Bay State Rd.

Floors: 8

Number of Occupants: 418

Bathrooms: 1 shared bathroom per suite

Coed: Yes

Room Types: Suite style with attached double rooms or a double with an attached triple

Special Features: Music room, stage, and dance floor, dining room, mail room, activity room, fitness room, laundry room, pool table, games room, public bathrooms, smoking room with a television, study space, and a bike rack

Residents: Under- and upperclassmen

The Towers

140 Bay State Rd.

Floors: Two 9-story buildings

Number of Occupants: about 1,000

Bathrooms: Common per floor

Coed: Yes, by floor

Room Types: Double-occupancy

Special Features: dining hall, computer lab, study rooms, and music practice rooms

Residents: Underclassmen

West Campus Complex

(Claflin, Sleeper, and Rich)

273, 275, 277 Babcock St.

Floors: Three buildings with 13 floors each

Number of Occupants: 1,776

Bathrooms: Communal baths, one per wing

Coed: Yes, with separate wings per floor. Single-sex floors are available

Room Types: Single-, double, triple-, and quadruple-occupancy rooms

Special Features: Next to Case Athletic Center (with Olympic-sized pool, ice-skating rink, fitness room, basketball courts, tennis courts, and saunas), cinema room, music practice rooms, smoking room, computer lab, dining hall, games rooms, laundry rooms, and mail rooms

Residents: Underclassmen

Bay State Road Brownstones

Floors: 4-5

Number of Occupants: 12-72 residents

Bathrooms: Communal per floor, or in suites

Coed: yes

Room Types: double-, triple-occupancy rooms, suites, and some quads

Special Features: Views overlooking Bay State Road and the Charles River, no security

Residents: Upperclassmen

South Campus Brownstones

Buswell, Carlton, and Beacon Streets, and Audobon Court on Park Dr.

Floors: Varies

Number of Occupants: 14-64 residents per building, with 1,800 residents total

Bathrooms: Varies per building

Coed: Yes

Rooms Types: Single-, double, triple-, and quadruple-occupancy rooms, and suites

Special Features: Computer resource room, fitness room, laundry room, television room, and lounges

Residents: Upperclassmen

University-Owned Apartments

The majority is located in the South Campus area, along Buswell Street, Arundel Street, Mountfort Street, St. Mary's Street, and Park Drive. There are also some on Bay State Road, Commonwealth Avenue, at the Hamilton House, and the Student Residence at 10 Buick Street.

Bed Type

Twin extra-long for all beds. In some of the dorms, there are bunk-beds available. BU also sells "Rack Raisers," available in various sizes to loft your bed.

Available for Rent

Micro-fridges

Cleaning Service?

The Physical Plant takes care of all of the cleaning services at BU. Public spaces are kept clean daily, as are communal bathrooms in the large dormitories. There is no private room cleaning service that is provided by BU.

What You Get

Dormitories

Each student receives a bed, desk (with storage space), chair, closet, dresser, Ethernet port, phone line, and mirror.

Apartments

Each student receives a bed, kitchen facilities, bathrooms, living area furnishings, desk chair, eating table and chairs, closet space, dresser, Ethernet port, telephone line, and mirrors.

Students Speak Out On...
Campus Housing

"Warren Towers is where a lot of freshmen live their first year, and it's not that great, but it's awesome for socialization. West Campus has more of a campus feel and it's across from the field."

Q "The dorms that you will likely get as a freshman (Warren Towers or West Campus) are like most **freshman dorms— they're small and cramped**. I guess they are part of the college experience, though. Some of the nicer ones that you could later get into are Shelton, Myles, and the best one by far, the Student Village, (but most people have no chance of getting into it, ever)."

Q "Warren is a pretty common dorm for freshmen. I suggest living there to meet people. But all **students strive to get into South Campus**, the Student Village and the brownstones. South Campus and the brownstones have no security, so anything goes, but you still have RAs. The Student Village is very nice, and it has air-conditioning and private rooms."

Q "**Definitely avoid Warren Towers**. It's where most freshmen get put, and it's a hellhole. But it is the best for freshmen because it's small, and you get to know everyone on your floor really well. Also, there are the brownstones, which are renovated and very nice. It's kind of hard to make a lot of friends if you start out there, and it's hard to get into them, but if you can, go for it! West Campus is really far away from the main campus, unless you're in the College of General Studies."

Q "The dorms are decent. Warren Towers is okay; it's very convenient due to its location. Plus, you can make a lot of new friends since its three towers are connected together and house about 1,400 students in all. If you're lucky, you can get an awesome view of the Boston skyline. **All the nice dormitories are located in West Campus**, but you'd be pretty far from your school, at least a 15-minute walk from the main part of the campus. The Towers are not coed within floors. All of the girls on one floor, and all guys on another floor."

Q "Definitely avoid Warren Towers if you can. Unfortunately, most freshmen end up there. I lived in the West Campus dorms for three years, and they're okay. **The Student Village is the best**. They are new apartments, but they're so hard to get into. South Campus is nice. It's all apartments, and there are no guards."

Q "**Dorm life sucks**. Get out of the dorms as soon as you can. BU dorms are the worst on the planet, so my advice: don't give them more money than you already are. Get off campus, where you can be a real person again."

Q "Dorm life is no fun. Honestly, it is really horrible. **Security guards just make living in the dorms a drag**, a big fat drag. We hate them; they hate us. It's normal, I guess. But you should always avoid stumbling in when you're not conscious of what you are doing. Otherwise, it can be a mess. Trust me, I've seen it. For freshmen, the dorms stink; you get tiny rooms with a lot of people all stuffed together. I mean come on, the hallways are wider than the rooms themselves, and doesn't that mean anything? Anything!"

Q "Avoid the dorms; especially Warren Towers, try to **get kicked out at all costs**. This is advice that you should take seriously . . . by any means necessary, I tell you."

Q "Dorm life is exciting at first, and then it starts to suck after you go visit friends who already moved off because then you get jealous. I had a great time in West Campus (it gives you that campus feel that you can't ordinarily get from BU). I guess Warren is a great place if you're a freshman, because you meet lots of people. Myles is nice, Shelton has great rooms, but I haven't been to Danielson because it's too far away, and the **Bay State brownstones are fabulous** (pray for them)."

Q "Dorms are bad, the scene is lame. **It is impersonal, overcrowded, severely regulated**, small, and the communal spaces get trashed daily by the inhabitants. Try to go for smaller buildings like The Towers, South Campus, and Bay State Road to avoid some of these problems."

Q "**Don't ever live in 1019 if you are a freshman**. There is no socializing whatsoever in those dorms. I think that West Campus is the best option. You make good friends because it is the only place with a campus atmosphere. As pathetic as it is, it works. Don't live in Warren Towers, it is just an awful zoo . . . but that is just what I heard."

The College Prowler Take On...
Campus Housing

When my letter arrived in the mail announcing my housing assignment at BU during the summer prior to my freshman year, I was concerned at best. I was living in West Campus (the farthest possible location from my classes), on an all-girls, non-smoking floor. This was not good, I told myself. As it turned out, however, West Campus is a great place to live freshman year. It is the only area with a grassy spot to hang out in, and it is located far enough away from campus to escape the incessant motion of daily life. Kids are often hanging out outside, playing guitar, talking, and generally interacting with one another—a sight rarely seen in city campus life. The dorm is also situated next to the football field, which is the perfect spot to play in on snow days, sleep on clear nights, or kiss on the 50-yard line in the early morning.

Whatever you do, stay away from Warren Towers. It is the largest non-military dorm in the United States, and it is a freshman machine. It even resembles a factory in appearance—you have to see it to push the analogy all the way. If you have ever seen the Pink Floyd movie, *The Wall*, pay attention to the scene accompanying that very song—that is it exactly. Other, smaller dorms are usually a safe bet but tend to be more secluded from campus life. If you can get a hold of a brownstone, don't give it up. They are by far the nicest living on and (in many cases) off campus.

The College Prowler® Grade on
Campus Housing:
D+

A high Campus Housing grade indicates that dorms are clean, well-maintained, and spacious. Other determining factors include variety of dorms, proximity to classes, and social atmosphere.

Off-Campus Housing

The Lowdown On...
Off-Campus Housing

Undergrads in Off-Campus Housing:
26%

Average Rent For:
Studio: $950 per month
1 BR Apt.: $1100 per month
2 BR Apt.: $1500 per month
4 BR Apt.: $2800 per month

Best Time to Look For a Place:
Get yourself organized around February to ensure a spot in a nice place.

Popular Areas:
Allston/Brighton
Brookline
Boston
Cambridge

For Assistance Contact:
Off-Campus Services
http://www.bu.edu/ orientation/offcampus/
(617) 353-3555

Students Speak Out On...
Off-Campus Housing

"Mostly upperclassmen live off-campus, because when you're a freshman, you want to hang around and meet people in the dorms."

Q "There are a lot of apartments around, but **finding a cheap one near campus can be a little tricky**. If you want one, you can find one without too many problems; you just have to look around. A lot of juniors and seniors eventually move off campus to avoid the guest policy and get cable (that's one thing that really sucks about BU dorms—no cable TV)."

Q "Most people don't move off campus until junior year. **Apartments are usually run-down and very expensive**. There are decent on-campus choices, especially the new buildings."

Q "Boston and **the suburbs are great for college housing**. You can find apartments both off campus and in the suburbs. Public transportation is always convenient for traveling if you live off campus."

Q "BU offers apartment-style housing, but mostly upperclassmen live there. If you really want to stay off campus, there are apartments located outside West Campus and outside South Campus. **Prices range from around $600 to $1400 a month per person.**"

Q "It's expensive, I'll tell you that. **The best place to get an apartment off campus, in my opinion, is Brookline**. It's a five-minute T ride from campus, and it's a great neighborhood, but like I said, it's expensive. I'm paying around $700 a month for a four-person apartment (that's per person), so it's pretty rough. Get out early if you're looking for rooms though, because there is always a rush for off-campus housing."

Q "**Off-campus housing seems easy to find**. Real estate in Boston is pretty expensive, though. It's fairly convenient because BU isn't really a campus, so you can live in off-campus housing and still be on-campus."

Q "Honestly, I think you'd be a fool to think that living on campus is better. First off, **living almost anywhere except for BU dorms is usually cheaper**. Off-campus housing also includes the conveniences of no security guards, or security tapes for that matter. And of course, the RAs—they'll undoubtedly piss you off, but if you get off campus, you're good to go. So concerning the question as to whether it is worth it or not to move off campus, it would definitely be worth it. In fact, it'd be stupid not to move off campus (unless you have to stay for financial aid or a scholarship, but that's just another BU control mechanism)."

Q "Personally, I wanted to stay on campus for my sophomore year because I was still meeting my friends and getting into the swing of things. I definitely would have wanted to move off by junior year. **Rent is pretty expensive, but so is living on campus**, so you can convince your parents with a bunch of numbers you threw together for your monthly budget that it's actually cheaper to live off (who knows if it is, really, but it's definitely worth it). But if you move off and decide you don't like it and want to come back on, BU gets very upset with you, and you'll probably have a tough time. Odds are, though, that you'll want to stay off."

The College Prowler Take On...
Off-Campus Housing

The consensus is that campus life is a benefit to your social life for freshman year. After that, it is time to move out. If freedom is an issue, and you intend to have visitors from off campus for overnight stays, the visitor policies can be really stifling. Partying is notoriously difficult in on-campus living, and if you are looking for privacy, off-campus housing is the only way to go.

My suggestion: move off campus after freshman year. I was forced to sleep on the field on several occasions because I neglected to set up a visitor request three days in advance. The discipline for "improper behavior" typically depends on the RAs, and brownstones are significantly less strictly upheld than the larger dorms. Specialty housing also includes its own specific restrictions concerning residents and guests. Moving off campus is a completely different lifestyle (read: freedom). But if money is tight, or you are supporting yourself, living is extremely expensive. Rent runs around $700 per month for a room. If you have the means, however, it is well worth it and really easy to find. There tends to be a moving explosion all over Boston on August 31st and September 1st, because that is when all of the leases turn over. If it is at all possible, try to move your stuff the day before the chaos begins.

B+

The College Prowler® Grade on
Off-Campus
Housing: B+

A high grade in Off-Campus Housing indicates that apartments are of high quality, close to campus, affordable, and easy to secure.

Diversity

The Lowdown On...
Diversity

Native American:
Less than 1%

White:
72%

Asian American:
13%

International:
7%

African American:
2%

Unknown:
1%

Hispanic:
5%

Out-of-State:
77%

Political Activity

Political groups on campus tend to be more prevalent on campus during times of political distress in the world. Due to the recent events in the U.S., the political scene has dramatically increased in visibility. The GSU held several events, joining students for Palestine with students for Israel in open public debates and discussion.

Gay Pride

BU has been in the spotlight for the surprisingly conservative views of the administration. While no student group within the University at the college level of education has been abolished, the gay activist group at the BU Academy (a high-school functioning under BU's administration—a breeding ground for potential applicants), was banned from operation in 2003. According to former BU President John Silber, these students were simply "too young" to explore any sexuality, let alone of the gay variety. This move brought a lot of negative attention to the University, as a gay professor in the Physical Education department resigned in protest of the ban. In general, however, there sometimes seem to be more gay men on campus than straight ones. The lesbian scene is slightly more concealed, but definitely prevalent. And Boston tends to be extremely tolerant to all forms of sexuality.

Economic Status

BU students span a wide range of economic backgrounds; however, the majority of students are middle- to upper-class.

Minority Clubs

There is a club or organization working to represent nearly every minority that is found on campus. While some are certainly more visible than others, the amount of activity is the result of the effort put forth by the members of the individual group. Due to the size of the University, there is literally something for everyone.

Most Popular Religions

Catholicism is the most prevalent religion on campus. There are also quite a few Protestants, Jews, and students who claim no religious affiliation.

Students Speak Out On...
Diversity

> **"BU is known for having one of the most diverse student bodies in the nation. We have many foreign students and many ethnic and cultural backgrounds. If you want diversity, BU is the best around."**

Q "I would say there is a diverse population. BU has a big international population, but the **majority of people are from the tri-state area** (Massachusetts, New York and New Jersey)."

Q "Campus diversity is one of the things that drew me to BU. I believe that there is a mixture of students here from all different backgrounds and classes. **Gay, straight, white, black, Asian**—we have everyone here."

Q "**There are so many international students**, and they are so nice. My roommate was from Venezuela, and one of my best friends was from Argentina. There is someone for everyone at this school."

Q "BU is internationally diverse, but **it is less than three percent African American**. There is a large Asian population. In general, the student body is fairly liberal and accepting of all races, ethnicities, and sexual orientations."

Q "There are people literally from all over the world and all 50 states. **There is every religion** and ethnic group you could imagine."

Q "I have definitely met a lot of people from different states and different countries. There are also a lot of religions on campus and **a lot of religious activities**, so if you are religious at all, or want to meet people in the same religion, there are a lot of opportunities for that."

Q "I came from an almost all-white high school, and it was great to be surrounded by all ethnicities and backgrounds. It is such a **wonderful cultural experience**."

Q "Culturally, Boston University is very diverse. Overseas, it is an extremely popular university to attend, so **it attracts students from many continents** and countries around the world. Chances are, you will have several international students in every class, which provides for a much more dynamic and culturally-relevant discussion of the subjects."

Q "I am not much a part of the campus life, but I can tell you that there is diversity; it just requires you seeking it out. Boston University is an establishment in which being a number can hinder you if you are looking for an exploding campus life. The involvement in groups and organization is as **diverse as any large, respectable campus**. I, for one, have never been a snug social bug. I have learned to open up to people throughout the years, as it is essential to be who you are. Otherwise, you may become simply another graduate, cranked out from the BU industry."

Q "There are two kinds of people on campus: the children of rich parents, and those who can't stand the children of rich parents. There is BU's diversity. Practically the only minorities at the University are the international students, who tend toward the School of Management and BMWs. **Coming from New York City, diversity is something I miss**."

○ "The campus is very **diverse in both culture and personality**. Many foreign students from Europe, Asia, and the Middle East attend. BU greatly opened my eyes to these cultures and to new ways of looking at things and thinking about such issues on my own. No one should have a problem finding his or her niche—there is a group for everyone to run with."

○ "BU is not as diverse as the University purports, but if you take the right classes you will find that diverse opinions certainly abide. Also, in the last few years, more and more eclectic personalities have come to the University, which means the kids who listen to the hip music, the club music, the rap, the rock, the Phish hits, the classical; yeah, they are all at BU. As for ethnicity, **most of the kids are white**, but there are a lot of international kids, depending on what school or classes you are in. SMG (School of Management) attracts many international students because of the renowned programs that college offers. If you take an African American studies class, chances are that you will be in a class with a lot of African Americans, and the same goes for Asian studies classes."

The College Prowler Take On...
Diversity

According to statistics, the majority of the Boston University population is comprised of white, middle- to upper-class students. Nevertheless, many individuals that I spoke to regarding their opinions concerning diversity on campus reported a large amount of personal exposure to minority groups on campus. Due to the size of the University, even small percentages of students may seem like a whole lot of people. Depending on your classes, your participation in campus events, and choice of social scene, you may or may not feel the effects of the comparatively low percentages of minority groups.

As it turns out, BU has a good reputation established in other parts of the world. There are a large number of European students who attend BU, many of whom flock to the School of Management (SMG). Many of these individuals are found lining the perimeter of this building on any given day, clad in Gucci and D&G, smoking Marlboro Menthol 100s, and leaning against a newly waxed BMW: corporate America's young hopefuls.

B-

The College Prowler® Grade on

Diversity: B-

A high grade in Diversity indicates that ethnic minorities and international students have a notable presence on campus and that students of different economic backgrounds, religious beliefs, and sexual preferences are well-represented.

Guys & Girls

The Lowdown On...
Guys & Girls

Men Undergrads:
7,279 (41%)

Women Undergrads:
10,461 (59%)

Birth Control Available?

There is a Planned Parenthood in West Campus on Commonwealth Avenue. Planned Parenthood offers gynecological exams, all forms of birth control presently available (including free condoms), the emergency contraceptive pill (without an appointment), STD testing, abortion services, and family planning. Not only are all of the above available, but they are provided at an extremely low cost, because they operate on a sliding scale and will take insurance. For more information, you can call Planned Parenthood at (617) 616-1600.

Social Scene

Surprisingly, there is a lot less interaction in classrooms and around campus. It is generally not the place to meet people. On any given day, students are usually clumped together, in prepackaged social circles. It is much easier to meet people off campus, and after academic hours.

Hookups or Relationships?

Freshman year is a sexual explosion. Hooking up is the only way to go. After that, and especially once you start finding your scene, people tend to pair off, at least for a while. Many people date individuals that they met outside of campus life. By graduation, relationships either last, or they don't. Either way, expect drama. With all of the moving around and general dispersal of your social circle, it's not easy to deal with a serious relationship.

Best Place to Meet Guys/Girls

Out in Boston, around the town, and in the clubs—there are so many kids hanging out everywhere. If you can't find anyone, you are staying home way too often.

Did You Know?

Top Places to Find Hotties:
1. The Mugar Memorial Library
2. Any of the clubs downtown
3. Commonwealth Avenue
4. If you like the alternative scene, check out the "Crack-slab" on Newbury Street. All sorts of kids hang out around there. Or head out to Copley Square and chill on the grass, you are bound to get approached by a hottie or three.

Top Places to Hook Up:

1. Along the Charles River
2. In the Boston Public Gardens
3. Nickerson Field
4. After-hours parties
5. On the rooftops of most buildings on campus

Dress Code

Most kids attending BU keep up with fashion, often to an obnoxious degree. Sitting along the sidewalk of Commonwealth Avenue can often feel like a model runway. As soon as the winter breaks, no matter what the temperature, the girls and guys on campus shed their layers, exposing their recent acquisitions from the French Connection, Prada, Gucci, D&G, Armani Exchange, and othe designers. A favorite activity: sit on Commonwealth Avenue, directly in front of a dip or crack in the cement (for good results, try the one to the left of the Tsai Center at the College of Arts and Sciences). Due to the fact that over half of the student body clip-clops around in high heels, this provides for an exciting afternoon. There is nothing better than watching some self-enraptured BU girl trip in heels and then pretend like nothing happened. Trust me.

Students Speak Out On...
Guys & Girls

> **"There are lots of hot guys and girlies, but there are lots of snobs, too. Expect to get looked down upon if you're on financial aid, or if you're not a trust-fund baby."**

Q "I have about had my fill of the guys in Boston, but **there are definitely some hotties about**. Your best bet is to go for guys not at BU, but Boston College and Northeastern guys, for sure."

Q "The boys that are on campus are mostly very hot. The girls, if they are lucky enough to get one of the guys, are very protective, but **many of the girls have boyfriends** anyway. Other than that, there are always the other colleges in Boston."

Q "The girls on BU campus **dress in expensive clothes and wear high heels** all the time. They are constantly on their cell phones, they take three hours to get ready, they're annoying as hell, and they wear a lot of perfume. But that's just my opinion."

Q "The campus is about 60 percent girls, and 40 percent guys. So for us guys, it's really nice. **The females, for the most part, are hot**, yet some can be stuck-up. Overall, we are an attractive campus."

Q "The guys, for the most part, are pretty good guys; of course, there is a fair share of jerks, but that's just normal. The girls are great; I seem to like them a lot. I think that **the girls are definitely hot**. The guys, well, that would have to be in your own judgment."

Q ”People here are nice and, for the most part, attractive. **We have a tolerant campus, so we have a lot of openly gay students**.”

Q ”BU is approximately 60 percent girls and 40 percent guys, so it's kind of rough meeting a cute, heterosexual guy. There are some definite hotties, but there are so many pretty girls, and it's hard to really snag one, but it does happen, I assure you. There are so many other schools around too, so **inter-school dating is fairly common**.”

Q ”The guys and girls vary. Some are really hot and some are really not. However, a lot of the women are Prada-wearing Gucci pushers, and the guys are pretty much the same. However, you do find your niche, and there are so many people that it doesn't really matter. One thing: there are more women than men. A good number of the men are gay. I have been told **there is a drought of good, straight men** . . . keep that in mind.”

Q ”Another great thing about Sargent College (the School of Health) is that it is practically all-female (can you feel the sarcasm!). You have to know where to look if you're in a program like mine, but I've definitely met my share of cute boys. I've really made my lifelong friends at BU. **I feel lucky to have met the people I have**, and I'm meeting new people all the time. The best way is to just get involved with things you enjoy.”

Q ”BU has a 3:7 guy/girl ratio. That being said, there are two types of people at BU: those who deserve to be here and those who have rich mommies and daddies. The latter outnumber the former. So as you might expect, **there are a lot of people at BU who spend more time at the gym than hitting their books**, so there are a lot of good looking people around. I have to admit, I spend some time there myself (I, too, can be mildly fickle), and don't mind it 'cause there are a lot of fine lookin' ladies walkin' around. No comment on the guys.”

Q "There are lots of girls, and **way too few guys**! Of course, it is very easy to hook up; it is college after all, and the boys are seemingly just going nuts. Suitable mates, on the other hand, are definitely more difficult to come by. The effects of the low population of males, as compared to females is felt, but it's not the end of the world. There are plenty of places to go to seek out members of the opposite sex. Just step outside."

Q "Supposedly, there are more girls in the Boston area than guys. Since there are so many different colleges, universities, and programs in Boston, however, there are many different types of people who are drawn to the area. **It is not hard to meet someone with your interests** . . . you just have to know where to look."

Q "I am asexual. I believe that sex is overrated. However, BU certainly has its own runway-modeling extravaganza every day from the 600 to 800 blocks of Commonwealth Avenue. Unfortunately, **many BU students are constrained victims of fashion**."

Q "There is no finer place for one to find cheap, meaningless sex than within the confines of a college dormitory. **Hooking up is easy, for the good, the bad, and the ugly**. Anyone can get laid—ANYONE. But don't expect to find the love of your life as a freshman. It is all very much a forgotten fallacy."

Q "In general, **the guys are more of the "pretty boy" variety**. They are very concerned with their image and looking good in their designer clothes. The ladies are very good looking, but also not much for intelligence, or personality. There are some very good-looking people here, but looks can be deceiving."

The College Prowler Take On...
Guys & Girls

If you are a guy—especially (but not necessarily) if you have just a glimmer of personality, intelligence, or looks—you are way ahead. There are girls to go around, and around again. The student body is notoriously described by those both on and off campus as shallow and materialistic. This is obviously not universally accurate, but BU certainly serves up its fair share of these sorts of individuals.

Writing as a female, heterosexual, recent graduate, in a University populated by nearly 60 percent females, the selection of suitable mates is certainly slim. If the good ones aren't taken, they are usually gay. In fact, all of the relationships that I had throughout college were with people that I met off campus (yet another benefit of city living). Finding people at such a huge university is easy; finding your niche, however, takes some time. Move around, get away from the university setting, and be open to friendships (romantic or otherwise), wherever they might occur.

The College Prowler® Grade on Guys: C+

A high grade for Guys indicates that the male population on campus is attractive, smart, friendly, and engaging, and that the school has a decent ratio of guys to girls.

The College Prowler® Grade on Girls: B+

A high grade for Girls not only implies that the women on campus are attractive, smart, friendly, and engaging, but also that there is a fair ratio of girls to guys.

Athletics

The Lowdown On...
Athletics

Athletic Division:
Division I

Conference:
America East Conference
Hockey East (hockey)
Colonial Athletic Association
(wrestling)

**Males Playing
Varsity Sports:**
274 (4%)

**Females Playing
Varsity Sports:**
280 (3%)

School Mascot:
Rhett, the Boston Terrier

Colors:
Scarlet and White

Men's Varsity Sports:
Basketball
Cross-Country
Golf
Ice Hockey
Soccer
Swimming & Diving
Track & Field (indoor and
outdoor)
Wrestling

➜

Women's Varsity Sports:
Basketball
Cross-Country
Field Hockey
Golf
Lacrosse
Soccer
Softball
Swimming & Diving
Tennis
Track & Field (indoor and outdoor)
Rowing

Intramurals:
Basketball (3 on 3 and 5 on 5)
Beach volleyball
Flag football
Floor hockey
Soccer
Inner Tube Water Polo
Softball
Swimming
Tennis
Volleyball

Club Sports:
Badminton
Ballroom Dancing
Baseball (men's)
Cheerleading
Cycling
Dance Team (women's)
Dance Theatre Group
Equestrian
Fencing
Figure Skating
Gymnastics
Ice Hockey (women's)
Inline Hockey
Lacrosse (men's)
Rugby
Sailing
Shotokan Karate
Ski Racing
Snowboarding
Table Tennis
Tae Kwon Do
Ultimate Frisbee
Volleyball
Water Polo (women's)

Athletic Fields

BU Softball Field
A grass field playing facility that is used for various team practices

Nickerson Field
Acts as the facility for the men's and women's soccer, and women's lacrosse teams. It is a 10,412-seat "FieldTurf" facility. The former football field of Boston University was also once the Boston Braves National League Baseball Club, until it was purchased. Nickerson Field is also home to the Boston Breakers, which is the city's first professional women's soccer team.

Getting Tickets

The ticket office is located in the Case Athletic Center. For information on ticket sales, call (617) 353-3838.

Most Popular Sports

Hockey is definitely the most popular sport at BU. The crew team is also a big influence on campus.

Best Place to Take a Walk

Walk alongside the Charles River, either on the Boston side, or the Cambridge side. There are statues, gardens, bridges, and benches lining the water. During the day or at night, this is definitely the most picturesque area of the city. There is a bike/blading trail, as well as a pedestrian walk-way, plus tons of grassy places to sit and contemplate, play hacky sack, or read a book. Another good spot to walk is down the center of Commonwealth Avenue, which is lined with trees covered in Christmas lights year round. Best of all, the walk takes you straight through the city until you hit the Boston Public Gardens.

Gyms/Facilities

Track & Tennis Center

The newly-completed Track & Tennis Center holds the activities of the Terriers' men's and women's track and tennis teams, as well as a practice venue for other Boston University athletic teams, physical education, and intramural sports. This state-of-the-art, air-conditioned facility is approximately 83,000 square feet. It is built to accommodate national competitions, athletic events, and University functions.

Strength and Conditioning Facility

A 7,000 square-foot strength and conditioning facility holding eight power racks, eight Olympic lifting platforms, and a 2000-square foot speed and plyometric area.

The DeWolfe Boathouse

Serves the Boston University men's and women's crew teams. It has racks that hold 68 shells, 48 rigged 8s, 12 rigged 4'2, and 8 rigged pairs. It is equipped with locker rooms, a lounge, offices, and a large dock. It is located on the Cambridge side of the Charles River, and has an interior and exterior balcony for fans to watch.

Boston University Academic Support Program

Held in the Elliot H. Cole Academic Support Center, this program assists student-athletes in their academics, and is available to all varsity student-athletes. There are 10 desktop computers, all networked to the University and the Internet, four laptops, and a laser printer.

Case Gymnasium

This houses the Terrier men's and women's basketball and wrestling teams, with a 1,800-seat capacity equipped with theater-sized chair back seats on both sides.

Faneuil Pool

Houses the men's and women's swim teams, and is a six-lane, 25-yard pool that also includes a diving area that has two one- and one three-meter boards. There is seating for 200 fans.

Walter A. Brown Area Memorial Skating Pavilion

The pavilion has a capacity of 3,806, and serves as the home of the Boston University hockey team. It is considered one of the finest facilities of its kind in the nation.

Student Village

The new center of campus life, providing students with recreation, athletics, living, dining, and outdoor spaces. The Village will include a track and tennis center, state-of-the-art fitness and recreation center, and a dance theater.

Students Speak Out On...
Athletics

> "Hockey is huge, and the Beanpot is crazy. It all depends on whether or not you're into sports to begin with. Basketball was big this year. Anyone can start a team for IM sports; you just need to get enough people together."

Q "Hockey East! **You must attend a hockey game**. I never went to one until college, but they are a lot of fun."

Q "Varsity hockey is great. I haven't missed a home game yet, especially considering that we are nationally-ranked, and **most of our starting players go onto the NHL**. Intramural sports are really great, but you have to take the initiative to get involved with them. I actually work on campus as an intramural referee, and everyone has fun. There are more than five different sports in each of three different sessions."

Q "BU is not known really for sports. We don't have a football team (they got rid of it back in '83); our major sport is hockey. We are awesome at hockey, and almost every year we win the Beanpot (a competition between Boston College and BU), but that's about it. **Intramurals are big**, and most of my friends are on some kind of team."

Q "People love hockey . . . **basketball is really big, too**, but not nearly as big as hockey. There are a million and one IM sports to play. People love them; there is really good participation, and it's very easy to get involved."

Q "All varsity sports are Division I, but **hockey gets the largest turn out** in terms of fans who actually attend the games. Basketball would be the second largest, and we also have soccer teams. Our school spirit isn't on the level of UNC or Duke, but if you enjoy watching sports, you can attend all games for free. IM sports are available, as well, and they offer pretty much anything you might want to play. You have to attend an informational meeting where you sign up to play on a team."

Q "Honestly, sports have never been my thing. Therefore, I did not choose BU due to its athletic opportunities or facilities. **BU has a really well-respected hockey team**, but beyond that, I don't think that our sports have been too widely celebrated."

Q "**Sports are pretty much negligible at BU**, unless you are part of some genetic upper caste. The people that I have come across who play sports decided to do so out of necessity (usually scholarships), and later, they despised it. They did not have time to associate with, let alone befriend, those people who lacked the physical prowess to run around with balls and wrestle one another in loosely fitting Speedos."

Q "With the exception of hockey, sports are not a big aspect of BU. The hockey team (and what other sport do you really need?) is usually # 3 or #4 and has some great athletes that are worth watching. There are **also numerous intramural sports** and plenty of people playing them."

Q "BU is humongazoid. There will always be 'jocks' when there are universities to recruit them. If you want to establish a community within BU, sports is one venue to do it in. Here, hockey is the major source of attraction, and Case Gym can be the place to pick up some hotties. For those on campus who prefer not to engage in sports, **you will not be ostracized or considered a dork if you do not join the cheerleading squad or pep team**."

The College Prowler Take On...
Athletics

About half of the students interviewed were totally unaware of the athletic scene at BU. The remaining students pretty much agreed that there are a decent amount of athletic opportunities for those who are interested. The athletic facilities are rapidly improving with the new addition of the tennis and track center at the Student Village. There seems to be more attention being paid to BU athletics by the administration over the past two years.

Hockey is, by far, the most celebrated varsity sport at BU. There is a "Beanpot" game every year between BU and BC, which always escalates into a party. I was on the intramural ski team. It is pretty safe to say that we played far more than we skied. While BU is not a huge sport mecca, pretty much everything is offered, from Frisbee golf, to basketball, to snowboarding, to sailing. Except . . . there is no football team, so if that is your thing, your best bet is to look elsewhere.

B-

The College Prowler® Grade on
Athletics: B-

A high grade in Athletics indicates that students have school spirit, that sports programs are respected, that games are well-attended, and that intramurals are a prominent part of student life.

Nightlife

The Lowdown On...
Nightlife

Club and Bar Prowler: Popular Nightlife Spots!

An Tua Nua

835 Beacon St., Boston

(617) 262-2121

An Tua Nua is a lounge in the South Campus that is 19+ and offers weekly theme-oriented nights, like Goth and Industrial on Monday nights. An Tua Nua has been very popular because of its affordable drink prices.

Aria

246 Tremont St., Boston

(617) 338-7080

This is a new gay club downtown. Some nights have a dress code, and it is usually 21+.

Avalon

15 Landsdowne St., Boston

(617) 262-2424

This is one of the most popular clubs in the Boston area. Some nights vary from 19+ to 21+. Avalon has been known to attract top names, like Paul Oakenfold.

➡

Axis

13 Landsdowne St., Boston
(617) 262-2437

Axis is also an extremely popular club, offering live and alternative music, as well as more mainstream dance nights. It is located immediately next to Avalon. Most nights there is no dress code, call for more information. Axis is 19+ every night.

Bill's Bar

5 1/2 Landsdowne St., Boston
(617) 421-9678

Bill's alternates between 18+ and 19+ all week long. Bill's is used both as a lounge space, and a venue for concerts.

Club Café

209 Columbus Ave., Boston
(617) 536-0966

This well-known gay (male) bar downtown is 19+ most nights of the week, and brings together an American menu with a lounge/bar atmosphere.

Copperfield's Bar

98 Brookline Ave.
(617) 247-8605

Copperfield's, located next to historic Fenway Park, features Boston's hottest local talent. They provide some of the best original, cover, and college bands throughout New England. Open seven days a week with live entertainment Thursdays, Fridays, and Saturdays.

Dick's Last Resort

55 Huntington Ave., Boston
(617) 267-8080

This is a restaurant/bar that occasionally has live entertainment. The waiters are paid to be extremely rude to the customers. This is supposedly a good time.

Embassy

30 Landsdowne St., Boston
(617) 536-2100

This is another prototype European-style Landsdowne club scene. There are both 19+ and 21+ nights.

Felt

533 Washington St., Boston
(617) 350-5555

This is a trendy club downtown, offering drinks and pool to the more mainstream crowd. It is 21+.

Harper's Ferry

158 Brighton Ave., Allston
(617) 254-9743

This is a really chill place, with live R&B, jam bands, and funk. They also have dart tournaments and pool. It is always 21+, but no dress codes.

Karma Club

9 Landsdowne St.
(617) 421-9595

Eastern-themed 19+ dance club, which gives a touch of distinction from the typical Landsdowne St. scene.

The Kells

161 Brighton Ave., Allston

(617) 782-9082

The Kells has premier rock shows on Wednesday nights. and drum and bass on Tuesdays. There is also pool, darts, dancing, DJs and food. It is 21+ with no dress code.

Lupo's Heartbreak Hotel

239 Westminster St., Providence

(401) 272-5876

Yeah, it is a drive. But they have great shows almost every weekend, with pretty big names. If you have a car, check it out. The club is 21+ and it has no dress code.

Matrix

275 Tremont St., Boston

(617) 338-ROXY

Typical 19+ club scene with a dress code (no sneakers). The Matrix is attached to the Roxy, located in the Theatre District.

Middle East

472 Mass. Ave., Central Square, Cambridge

(617) 497-0576

Cool venue with three levels of live music and Middle Eastern food. The place is 18+, with occasional 21+ shows. But if you are going, remember your ID. Even for 18+ shows, they are extremely strict: no ID, no entrance.

Model Café

7 North Beacon St., Allston

(617) 254-9365

The Model has a '50s feel, showing new works by local artists, and offering home-style lunch and dinner specials, four beers on tap, accompanied by good music and a personal atmosphere. It is populated by a 21+ hip, punk, and mod crowd—no dress code. Lines for Model can get very long so be sure to arrive early.

O'Brien's Pub

3 Harvard Ave., Allston

(617) 782-9082

Irish style brewery in Allston; The pub is 21+, with no dress code.

Our House West

1277 Commonwealth Ave., Allston

(617) 782-3228

This is the big BU nightspot. It is 21+ at night, but the restaurant has no age restrictions during the day. It has comfy couches covered in pillows, foosball, pool, cheap food ($5 burgers in 11 varieties), board and card games, TV, and an easy-going attitude.

Paradise Lounge

969 Commonwealth Ave., Boston

(617) 562-8804

Offers live rock and DJs at the club, with a history of great musicians that have played with them. The lounge is more of the hip punk scene. (*Tip: it is really easy to sneak into shows undetected if you show up after the first hour or so. You enter the building before purchasing a ticket . . . so if you just walk by the ticket-taker, they usually won't stop you.)

Palladium

261 Main St., Worcester

(508) 797-9696

This venue holds big concerts in Massachusetts (Moe, Sound Tribe Sector Nine, Disco Biscuits). There is no dress or age restriction.

Phoenix Landing

512 Mass. Ave., Cambridge

(617) 576-6260

This is a small club/bar in Cambridge with a good atmosphere and a young crowd. There are good drum and bass and break beats on Thursdays. It is 21+ every night, but no dress code, and a really cheap cover.

Pour House Bar & Grille

909 Boylston St., Boston

(617) 236-1767

The Pour House is 21+ at night, with no age restrictions during the day. The atmosphere is one of the best of the restaurants/bars in the Boston area, and there is no dress code. The food and drinks are not only really good, but really cheap, as well.

Gypsy Bar

116 Boylston St., Boston

(617) 482-7799

With its dimly lit corners, inviting couches and plasma TVs tuned to the Fashion Channel, Gypsy Bar is the spot for a chic late-night rendezvous. DJs please European students by spinning international dance tunes

Roxy

279 Tremont St., Boston

(617) 338-ROXY

While the Roxy holds some of the best concerts in Boston (Ween, The Flaming Lips, and the Disco Biscuits were there), if you show up on any other night, it is more of the same well-dressed, overpriced, generic club scene. For live music there is no dress code and it is 18+, but most other nights are 21+ with no sneakers allowed.

Silhouette Lounge

200 Brighton Ave., Allston
(617) 254-9306

This lounge, a local favorite, is mainly populated by students and old men. Pool and darts are taken very seriously here. There is cheap food and drinks, and is 21+ every night with no dress code.

Sunset Grille and Tap

130 Brighton Ave., Allston
(617) 254-1331

There are about 300 different types of beer available every day. So if beer is your thing, this is the place to go. It is also a restaurant, so there are no age or dress restrictions, and the food is as good as the beer. Whatever you do, don't dare order a Bud Light with your meal. You will be made fun of by your waiter.

T.T. the Bear's Place

10 Brookline St., Central Sq., Cambridge
(617) 492-BEAR

T.T.'s offers live rock and roll, pinball, and a pool table. It is usually 18+ and doesn't have a dress code.

Venu

100 Warrenton St., Boston
(617) 338-8061

Venu is one of those clubs that varies by night. Some of the hottest young people in Boston show up at this club.

Vertigo

126 State St., Boston
(617) 723-7277

This is a small modern club with a good atmosphere, depending on the night you attend. Drinks tend to be a bit expensive. The age restrictions and dress codes vary by night. Check out Wednesday nights for good Psy-trance.

Who's On First?

19 Yawkey Way
(617) 247-3353

Stop in before the game for cold drinks, big screen TVs, great music and a crowd that knows what a good time is all about. Then come back after the game because when the lights go out in Fenway the dancing begins at Who's. With a great mix of classics you love and the newest music you wanna hear being played by one of the five House DJs.

Wonder Bar

186 Harvard Ave., Allston
(617) 351-COOL

This place is only a good time if you like that plastic, flashy, expensive feel of most posh city bars and clubs. While there is pretty good jazz, the vibe is obnoxiously unintelligent. The bar is 21+ and has a strict dress code.

Other Places to Check Out:

Jillians' Billiards Club
145 Ipswich St.

(617) 437-0300

Jillian's offers a great atmosphere for eating American food like burgers, sandwiches, and pizza, while hob-knobbing with celebrities such as Derek Jeter, Mark Walhberg, Clint Eastwood or Sean Penn. They have 55 pool tables, virtual games, and six full bars.

Rise
306 Stuart St.

(617) 423-7473

Rise is Boston's only after-hours club; with two levels and a diverse crowd, it's the place to hang after 2 a.m. when the rest of the city closes—plan ahead: it's a membership club.

Bars Close At:
2 a.m.

Primary Areas with Nightlife:
Landsdowne St.

Allston/Brighton

Cambridge (Mass Ave. area)

Chinatown/Theater District

Downtown

Cheapest Place to Get a Drink:

Pour House has 24 ounce Bruebaker's for only $2.

Favorite Drinking Games:

Kings

Beer Pong

Student Favorites

The majority of students prefer the more mainstream clubs located on Landsdowne Street (i.e. Karma, Avalon, Axis, Bill's Bar, Jillian's), or the Euro-trash scene that is scattered around the city (i.e. Aria, Pravda 116, Roxy). You should check out the live music scene at Paradise, Middle East, Harper's Ferry, House of Blues, or T.T. The Bear's. If you are into the electronic movement, try the Phoenix Landing (Thursday nights are drum and bass), Rise (open after-hours on Friday, Saturday, and Sunday for trance and house), Vapor (Saturday nights are house and progressive), and Vertigo (Wednesday nights are psy-trance).

As for the bar scene: Allston definitely has the best bars in the area. Our House, for example, is the BU meeting/breeding grounds. It is by far the cheapest way to go, and the best way to run into old friends. Avoid the Wonder Bar, unless you own your weight in Prada, and check out the Silhouette instead for darts and pool.

Useful Resources for Nightlife

If you go to *Google.com* and type in "Boston clubs," you will get several nightly listings of all of the clubs in the area. Be warned: hey are not always kept up-to-date. You might go to to Vapor expecting drum and bass, but find Asian karaoke night, instead. For live music, your source is *Jambase.com*; it has all of the festival and show listings for every state across the U.S. The *Weekly Dig* and *Improper Bostonian* are two free newspapers that will keep you up-to-date.

What to Do if You're Not 21

If you check the listings, most clubs regularly have 18+ nights, especially for special events/live music shows. Frat parties are always available for nighttime partying around campus (both at BU, and the other schools in the area). Apartment parties are literally everywhere, every night. Information about outdoor parties is usually spread by word of mouth (there are some fun ones that are thrown on the beach on Cape Cod).

The Other Side Cosmic Café

407 Newbury St., Boston

(617) 536-9477

Serves really healthy and interesting food, including fruit smoothies, brie, pear sandwiches, and beer. The atmosphere is really chill, and they are open pretty late.

Aquarium IMAX

Central Wharf, at the end of State St. T: Aquarium (Blue)

(617) 973-5200

The Aquarium has a new 3D IMAX theatre that is open after the exhibits close.

The Asylum

1592 Main St., Springfield

(203) 287-8398

The Asylum holds all of the major raves in the Massachusetts area. Various production companies throw parties at this venue once a month, and have hosted really big names in the electronic industry, across genres. There are four rooms, each with a different sound. Tickets for parties are sold around $25 and are available at Satellite Records on Massachusetts Avenue, on the corner of Newbury Street.

Frats

See the Greek section!

Students Speak Out On...
Nightlife

"Bars and clubs are really strict and tight, so if you have a fake ID, unless it's perfect, it probably won't work. But most clubs have a college night, which is dancing, and it's tons of fun. Ana Tua Nua, Copperfield's, and Who's on First? are the best."

"The clubs are mostly 19-and-over to get in, and on Saturdays, they're 21-one and over, but freshman always find a way to get in. They all close at 2 a.m., unlike any other city where places stay open until all hours. Anyway, the popular club street is Landsdowne Street. The clubs are called Karma, Avalon (all house, very Euro), Axis (house and techno, hip hop upstairs on Thursday), and Jillians' (mostly an arcade, 19 and over to get in). And then there are bars. Also, my other favorite place, which I used to promote for, is Bill's Bar. They play hip-hop on Tuesday nights—a very good scene if you like that kind of music. I never was interested in that, but if you are, it's a good place to go. The bar scene is a little different because there are tons of bars."

"Clubs are great. **They always offer specials and stuff**, too. If you know people who promote or work for a club, you can always get on a list and it is $10 instead of $15, and a lot of times there are free passes floating around. Avalon is really fun, and they have lots of great concerts every week, too."

Q "Although having a fake ID is a felony in Massachusetts, if you have one, you can get into a lot more clubs and bars. If you don't, there are still several places that have college night. They are 19-and-above, but if you are a girl and have a Boston University ID, they will usually let you in at eighteen. **The biggest club zone in Boston is Landsdowne Street**, which is practically on BU's campus, so if you like clubs, it's a good place to be."

Q "There are **no parties on campus because BU's dorm security is anal-retentive**. Everyone I know who tried to have even the most modest get-together freshman year got kicked out of housing. That is why I moved off campus. The clubs are pretty cool if you're going to a good show. I'm into punk and Indie music, but Boston doesn't really have much of an underground scene. Most of the good shows are usually in people's houses. I'm only 20, so I can't get into bars unless I'm playing in them, but some of them seem pretty cool. You can't smoke anywhere anymore, which is a drag."

Q "Boston is so expensive. But there are nights, many of them, during which your money, no matter how much you spent, will definitely be worth it. There are times when money doesn't really matter because the party is everywhere. **Sometimes the parties are taken outside to the streets**. I've even been in a riot in the neighborhoods by all the apartments; it was incredible, and people were destroying things. But in the end, everybody had a great time. I've heard there are some real phat clubs and what not, plus a lot of booze to be bought."

Q "I am a bit of a nerd, and therefore might not be the best authority on the party scene at BU. That said, however, from what I have heard, **the fraternity parties are actually rather torrid**, and not worth the trouble. Personally, I consider myself to be more of a homebody."

Q "**Parties on campus are usually not good**. Why? Because when you first come to BU wanting to go to a party, someone will usually send you to Gardner Street to some frat party, where there are a ridiculous amount of people, you pay five bucks for a single beer before the one keg meant for the entire student body is kicked. Plus, the crowd is pretty shallow and frat/sorority-ish (sorry if you like that sort of thing). It's so much more fun if you get a bunch of your friends together and party at one of their places. As far as being underage and in Boston, I always found the security pretty tight. But the farther you get away from campus, the easier it is to get a drink. If you like clubs and dancing, go to Landsdowne Street. Some of my favorite bars are in Allston: Our House West, Silhouette Lounge, and Model Cafè."

The College Prowler Take On...
Nightlife

Because the Greek aspect of campus life is lacking, students gather off campus at the large variety of clubs/bars/lounges that constitutes the nightlife of Boston. This brings several benefits to social living: you can interact regularly with students from other universities (Boston College, Emerson, Northeastern, MIT, and Harvard), as well as meet other individuals from the area, and you also have the benefit of incorporating so much more activity into a Friday night. This is a big step away from drunken nights spent trying to get closer to the keg.

Boston draws big names in music, the arts, and all forms of entertainment, providing ample opportunities for either a good party, or a cultural evening. Landsdowne Street tends to be the breeding grounds for typical club-goers. Check out more causal and eclectic venues like the Middle East, Paradise Lounge, Phoenix Landing, Venu, or Rise. Of course, if a well-spent night of drinking is your primary interest, rest assured that anytime you stick thousands of college students in a small area, there is plenty of that sort of fun to go around. Apartment parties are usually open to the public (for a few dollars), and just walking down Ashford Street on a Saturday is a sure bet for some heavy activity to show itself.

The College Prowler® Grade on

Nightlife: A-

A high grade in Nightlife indicates that there are many bars and clubs in the area that are easily accessible and affordable. Other determining factors include the number of options for the under-21 crowd and the prevalence of house parties.

Greek Life

The Lowdown On...
Greek Life

Number of Fraternities:	**Undergrad Men in Fraternities:**
7	3%
Number of Sororities:	**Undergrad Women in Sororities:**
9	5%

➜

Fraternities on Campus:

Tau Epsilon Phi
Zeta Beta Tau
Kappa Sigma
Lambda Chi Alpha
Lambda Phi Episilon
Phi Iota Alpha
Sigma Chi

Sororities on Campus:

Alpha Delta Pi
Alpha Kappa Alpha
Alpha Kappa Delta Phi
Alpha Phi
Delta Delta Delta
Delta Gamma
Gamma Phi Beta
Sigma Delta Tau
Sigma Kappa

Other Greek Organizations:

Kappa Kappa Psi, a coed band fraternity

Psi Chi, the national honor society for psychology

Pi Sigma Alpha, students interested in government and politics

Alpha Eta Mu Beta, biomedical engineering organization

Phi Alpha Delta, fraternity for pre-law students

Alpha Phi Omega, a coed community service fraternity

Golden Key Honor Society, a Greek honor society

Students Speak Out On...

Greek Life

"Greek life is eight percent of the student body, and not very dominating at all. Frat parties are lame. Sororities are there if you like them, but there are no houses because of Massachusetts state law."

"Fraternities and sororities are not allowed on campus at BU, so **Greek life is very small**. It tends not to dominate the social scene, but BU is known as a bit of a party school."

"Greek life is only a small percentage of the population. I, myself, am in a sorority, and **it is a great way to meet tons of people all at once**. Formal rush is in January for freshmen. There are nine sororities and about as many fraternities."

"Greek life is something that I'm not into; I don't do that whole scene. **BU is so big that nothing really dominates the whole social scene**, per se. Your social scene is something that depends on who you are and what you're into."

"The Greek life is there if you want it, but it definitely does not dominate the social scene. I think that is true for most urban schools. You will have plenty to do off campus, and **a lot of people prefer to explore Boston's nightlife instead of the frats**. If you want Greek life, it's there, and those who attend on a regular basis enjoy them. It's not really my scene, though."

Q "Greek life is very minimal at BU. There are a couple of frats and sororities, but not a lot of people join. **Frats usually have parties on Thursday and Saturday nights, which are sometimes fun** and sometimes really lame. But, it's another great way to meet people."

Q "Greek life is practically **non-existent unless you seek it out**. We do have frat houses, and we do have sororities (they don't have houses, though, because there's some ridiculous ancient law in Massachusetts that says that if there are more than seven women living in a single residence it's considered a 'brothel' and it's illegal)."

Q "I have had no experience with BU's Greek life, **but it does exist**. There are also a few MIT frat houses on the BU campus.'"

Q "**There isn't much**; it all depends on where you live. If you live on West Campus, then you'll go to more frat parties because that's where the BU frats are."

Q "I think the Greek life is like six percent . . . it is really bad; no one is really joining, and **the rush is a joke**. You definitely do not have to be in the Greek life to have fun."

Q "As far as social life is concerned, **being a part of the Greek system has endlessly expanded my social circle**. Of course, there is a little bit of competition between chapters, but I have tons of friends (including my best friend in the entire world) in other chapters. I also have tons of friends that are not in sororities or fraternities. I am able to spend time with everyone I want to. I never had to give up old friends for Gamma Phi. I've also never had to compromise my grades (they actually got better), or any other activities. I cannot say enough about how great being in a sorority is."

Q "If you're on East Campus, then **you'll probably end up at MIT frats** which are good. Greek life doesn't really dominate at BU because there are so many people."

Q "Boston University and the student population in the Boston area are both so large that the **Greek life definitely gets lost in the mix**. Those who seek it out will find it, and others who steer clear of that sort of thing will have no problem avoiding it. Unless you consciously choose to become involved with the Greek system, you normally never even hear about it."

Q "**There is a small Greek crowd**, but it is there if you are looking for it. There is plenty of Greek life in between all of the universities in the area. I do not recommend it unless you want it, but then, that's a shame."

Q "As for Greek life, **it is totally non-existent**. Greek is an expletive, unless we're talking classics."

Q "Greeks are present at BU, but not overwhelming. I would say you really need to look around to find a frat. You are certainly not obligated to be in one to have friends, but people seem to be pretty close with their brothers. Mostly, the **frat houses are just places to go and party** on weekends."

Q "Greek is not life on campus . . . it is for a small percentage of students, but it is not considered the coolest or best kind of student organization to get involved with. Other organizations and kids throw parties that are just as good, if not exponentially better than the Greeks. Also, many of the Greeks follow the dumb stereotypes of the MTV reality shows . . . keep that in mind when pledging. **It dominates the scene for the unimaginative**."

The College Prowler Take On...
Greek Life

For those who are looking for it, Greek life does exist. It does not, however, dominate the social scene as it tends to do at other U.S. colleges. For many students attending BU, the lack of a prevalent Greek scene on campus is a welcomed benefit of student life. The truth is that Boston offers far more outside of campus grounds, and an overwhelming Greek population would have little influence on the dispersed student body. For some, Greek life is the alternative to a real social life. As one student commented, "it dominates the scene for the unimaginative." It seems to have been created for individuals who are attending small schools or schools located in more remote areas. For many, this scene is simply unnecessary here.

It's widely believed that, according to Boston law, more than seven unrelated females living in the same space are considered to be running a house of prostitution (though the "blue law" that designates this was actually repealed in 1984). Regardless, there are no sorority houses, either on or off campus. While fraternities do not share the same logistical problems, the Greek life constitutes only approximately eight percent of the student population.

The College Prowler® Grade on
Greek Life: C

A high grade in Greek Life indicates that sororities and fraternities are not only present, but also active on campus. Other determining factors include the variety of houses available and the respect the Greek community receives from the rest of the campus.

Drug Scene

The Lowdown On...
Drug Scene

Most Prevalent Drugs on Campus:
Alcohol
Pharmaceuticals
Marijuana
Ecstasy
Cocaine

Liquor-Related Referrals:
468 on campus
9 on public property

Liquor-Related Arrests:
10 on campus
8 in dormitory
35 on public property

Drug-Related Referrals:
19 on campus
8 on public property

Drug-Related Arrests:
15 on campus
7 in dormitory
9 on public property

➜

Drug Counseling Programs:

The Boston University Counseling and Wellness Center

19 Deerfield St. 2nd floor
(617) 353-3540

The Danielson Institute

185 Bay State Rd.
(617) 353-3047
daninst@bu.edu

Student Health/Mental Health Services

881 Commonwealth Ave.
(West entrance)
(617) 353-3575

Students Speak Out On...
Drug Scene

"Not many people do drugs, but I might not know all that much about it because I lived on the pre-med floors of Warren. There is some drug use, but not much."

"There's nothing heavy and open. **There is stuff around if you want** it I guess, but it's not thrown in your face."

"I never saw a lot of drugs. I know **weed is common**, but I don't smoke, so I don't know where to get it or who to get it from. If you don't choose to hang around it, you probably won't see it. As far as anything else, if you don't look for it, you probably won't see it."

"**Drugs don't seem to be a big problem**, but alcohol is always a battle for the administration."

"I don't do it, but it's the usual. **Alcohol is big, of course**. Weed is the biggest of the drugs, then I would say E, coke and K. Everything is here; it is a city. The University and the police are very strict though, so party hearty, but be safe and smart."

"**E, coke, pot and alcohol** are the big ones."

"I stay away from that stuff, but **you can find it if you're looking hard enough**. It's there, but not if you don't want it to be."

"If you want drugs, you can get them. **If you don't like them, then they'll never cross your path**. It's just that easy."

Q "Drug scene . . . I prefer alcohol myself, but BU has plenty of people who enjoying smoking weed once in a while, and plenty of people who don't. I have a lot of friends who smoke on a regular basis and a lot of friends who have never touched the stuff. There is also a contingent of kids at BU who do E and coke, but for the most part, **alcohol and weed are the two main drugs**."

Q "**I only know of the pot situation**. I didn't smoke it, but a lot of people on my floor did. It's there if you want it."

Q "Honestly, I can say that **I know more kids that use drugs recreationally than those that do not**. Never, however, have I witnessed someone being forced to try something that they did not want to do themselves. If drugs are something that you wish to do, they are not hard to come by, depending on the varying supply."

Q "The drugs scene on campus, itself, is not very big. There is always pot and a **ridiculous amount of smuggling of alcohol going on**. However, the harder drugs are not around campus as much as they are around certain circles. Also, allow me to extend a friendly reminder not to accept sketchy hook ups—it's just safer, trust me."

Q "**The drugs are just as common around BU as the sex**. While the former certainly aren't as cheap as the latter, they tend to be slightly more meaningless."

Q "**You will definitely encounter drugs at BU**. While not needing to do them to fit in, many kids seem to be into them and experimenting with all sorts of things (be careful, as I have seen it both screw people up and open their minds to new things)."

Q "If you want drugs, you can find them, but **do not get caught with them**. There is a reason kids live off campus. Get the point?"

The College Prowler Take On...
Drug Scene

Ah, yes, the drug scene. It is pretty readily agreed by most students that drugs are certainly a prevalent and available source of recreation on campus and off. No one, however, felt that this sort of activity was so rampant that it put a strain on campus life. The drug scene, while visible, is easily avoidable. Students stressed the ability to choose your own scene. It is really easy to find people who are into, or not into, just about everything. The drugs that were most readily seen on campus were alcohol, marijuana, cocaine, and ecstasy. Many also noted that pharmaceuticals are often considered a "useful tool" for completing schoolwork or distressing from academic life.

As in any city, there are fluctuations in what is available, and whatever is circulating tends to be overpriced. To be brief, various social circles have their various social vices. Pick and choose as you see fit.

The College Prowler® Grade on

Drug Scene: C+

A high grade in the Drug Scene indicates that drugs are not a noticeable part of campus life; drug use is not visible, and no pressure to use them seems to exist.

Campus Strictness

The Lowdown On...
Campus Strictness

What Are You Most Likely to Get Caught Doing on Campus?

- Smoking pot
- Burning incense
- Smoking cloves in dorm rooms
- Drinking underage
- Public urination
- Noise violation
- Violating guest policy

Students Speak Out On...
Campus Strictness

"Campus police do very little. BU is very strict about marijuana, though. You can get kicked out of housing if two resident advisors smell it; it is a pretty strict rule. Everyone who drinks gets away with it if they are smart about it."

"RAs make rounds every night, and if you're caught drinking or doing anything else in your room, you are in serious jeopardy of being kicked out of housing. My friends and I would drink in the rooms, but **you have to be careful and responsible** in order not to get caught."

"If you're caught with either drugs or alcohol, you're screwed, but if you're 21, you can have a certain amount of liquor in your room. **If they catch you, you get a judicial hearing**, and you might get kicked out of housing. People do smoke pot and drink in the dorms, though—it's common."

"**The drinking policy isn't too tight**. Most people get an alcohol violation at some point or another, but it isn't a big deal. The drug policy is pretty strict, though."

"The BUPD is very strict about drugs and underage drinking. At times, they **stake out places such as liquor stores to see if under-aged students are buying alcohol**. But if you don't make a scene in public or cause any commotion, they will leave you alone."

Q "BU has some pretty strict drinking rules, but **it is mostly RAs who enforce them**, and you have to be pretty dumb to get caught."

Q "If you use drugs or drink alcohol and get caught, you will be written up, have a letter sent to your parents, and possibly be kicked out of housing, or more likely put on probation. All violations are written up by the RAs, and the hall directors handle each case and determine the disciplinary action. If it is a major incident, BU judicial plays a role. The bottom line: don't be dumb! **If you are caught, you will be written up**."

Q "In my experiences with the campus police and security guards, I have typically found them to be extremely strict as compared with other schools that my friends attend. Security really seems to be ever-present. They are always around, and **they are equipped with magic noses**."

Q "On campus drugs and **drinking policies are very strict, and they are no joke**, as they mean what they say with absolutely no exceptions. I learned this the hard way. Before classes had even begun my freshman year, I had already lost my on-campus housing privileges. One afternoon, I had decided to smoke a few joints in a dorm with a friend that I had met at orientation. We thought that we had gotten away with it, but about an hour later, however, we were sitting there in his room, chilling, listening to music, when a knock came at the door. The RAs said they smelled marijuana emanating from the room. They took a look around and found no hard evidence that we were smoking pot, aside from the smell. Two weeks later, both he and I were asked to leave campus housing. If you want to keep your housing . . . there are plenty of opportunities to party off campus."

Q "I have never been in any direct confrontation with the forces that be. Yet, they do not seem to be extremely lenient on anything in particular. May I remind you **we are residing in a Puritan state of America**."

Q "It's **Orwellian**."

Q "There are very strict rules, and they are definitely enforced the most severely in the dorms. Keep in mind that **the first few weeks have a lot of busts to send a message to the new students** in on-campus housing. After that, it settles down."

Q "Campus police are very strict, but **no one said you couldn't party**. Just don't be stupid and have five loud kids who can't hold their liquor partying in your room."

The College Prowler Take On...
Campus Strictness

Playing it smart seems to be the best bet. Stick to your limits, stay far from University buildings when you expect to party, and if things tend to get out of control, make sure you are not in the dorms. Getting caught with drugs (or alcohol, if you are underage) may result in academic probation or removal from housing on campus. What you get away with depends largely on your housing assignment. Rules vary in strictness from dorm to dorm, and RA to RA.

When I was a student, my RA was extremely lenient with all of the students living on the floor. Do not, however, expect to be let off. I know plenty of students who were handled with much less concern. Be extra careful early on in the academic year. BU tends to "send a message" to students, before things even get rolling.

The College Prowler® Grade on

Campus Strictness: B-

A high Campus Strictness grade implies an overall lenient atmosphere; police and RAs are fairly tolerant, and the administration's rules are flexible.

Parking

The Lowdown On...
Parking

Approximate Parking Permit Cost:

Blue: (day/commuter)
Semester 1: $295.80
Semester 2: $348.00
Cumulated: $643.00
Summer: $261.00

Orange: (overnight)
Semester 1: $404.43
Semester 2: $475.80
Cumulated: $880.25
Summer: $365.85

White: (evening)
Semester 1: $43.00
Semester 2: $43.00
Cumulated: $83.23
Summer: $43.00

BU Parking Services:

(617) 353-2160
George Sherman Union,
775 Commonwealth Ave.,
2nd Floor
http://www.bu.edu/parking
Office is open Monday–Friday
9 a.m.–5 p.m.

Common Parking Tickets:

Expired Meter: $25

No Parking Zone: $10-$30

Handicapped Zone: $50

Fire Lane: $40

Student Parking Lot?

There are several student lots around campus. Depending on the parking permit you have, accessibility to each lot varies.

Freshmen Allowed to Park?

Yes

Parking Permits

You can either purchase a parking permit online, by mail, over the phone, or by going directly to the Office of Parking at the GSU during operating hours. It is relatively easy to get, assuming you have the cash to spend. Prices are steep. If you live off campus, the best way to go is to register your car in Massachusetts and get a resident permit parking pass for your car. It is only about $15, and allows you to park on the street in the area in which you live. All you need is your valid registration, license, and proof of residency. Then again, students have survived (with difficulty) without a permit.

Did You Know?

Best Places to Find a Parking Spot

If you do not have a permit and you are looking for a spot on campus, you will rarely find a space on Commonwealth Avenue during your first sweep. Be prepared to go around in circles for a few minutes before finding a decent spot, but because they are lined up one after another, something will most likely eventually pop up. If you are headed to class, taking your car is rarely a time saver. Your first reflex may be to hop in the car instead of waiting for the T, but don't. The virtue of the T is that it always comes. It's not the same for parking. Sometimes, if you check Cummington Street or Bay State Road, there are some open spots. Also, the further away from central campus, the easier it is to park; check down by Kenmore Square.

Good Luck Getting a Parking Spot Here!

It is basically impossible to find a spot anywhere around east campus on a Red Sox game day. Fenway Park is right around the corner from BU, and there are hoards of people . . . and their cars. Don't get stuck looking for a spot anywhere near there on game day, unless you are prepared to pay the 20 bucks for parking.

Students Speak Out On...
Parking

"There are parking lots, but it's pretty expensive to park your car all year. There really is no reason to have a car in Boston; public transportation is easy and affordable."

Q "I recommend that you not bring a car. There is no room for parking, and a **very small number of passes are issued** for about $450 a year."

Q "Parking and driving in Boston is kind of a hassle in general (the drivers are crazy). So unless you have a specific reason for bringing a car, you really don't need one. **You can get pretty much anywhere by walking or taking the T**, which runs right along BU's campus. You can basically get out right in front of your dorm."

Q "**It's really expensive to park, and it's terrible to drive in Boston**. If you need to get a parking sticker, get one; it's easier to park in lots and the garage at Warren Towers than it is to park on the street."

Q "**The police ticket like crazy**, and it's really expensive to have a car. "

Q "I can't really suggest bringing a car to Boston. **We have terrible traffic**, aggressive drivers, and we have the T system. It's usually easier just to walk or take the T to wherever you want to go."

Q "Do not bring a car! Parking in Boston is a disaster, especially while they're doing major construction on campus. The T will take you anywhere in the city you want to go, and even to the towns around the city. And there are cabs. **BU students walk a lot**, too; it is very easy to get places by walking in Boston."

Q "Parking in Boston is non-existent. I have never brought my car to Boston, as you really do not need it. I guess you can buy a parking permit to have the privilege to park in a BU lot, but it doesn't guarantee you a spot, and **it is mad expensive**. Also, if you choose to park on the street, you are lucky if you can park remotely close to your destination. Public transportation is the way to go in Boston."

Q "The parking is overpriced and hard to find. The public transportation is really efficient, however. Don't bother trying to go out at night to clubs with your car. Cabs are around all night, and the **buses run until 2 a.m. on the weekends**."

Q "Do not even consider double-parking or leaving your car illegally parked even with your hazards on, even just for a second. They will find you. **The meter maids are always just out of view**."

Q "Boston is crowded, and unless you have a parking space, it is **very hard to find a spot**. There will be many times when you are late for class because you were out looking for a spot, times when you'll be ticketed because you thought the space was legal and it wasn't, times when you're towed, and times when you must drive back to your parents house to find a spot to park. I live in Boston and don't use a vehicle here—the T is excellent anyways! Just use that."

Q "My roommate got 14 tickets last semester. **Do not bring a car**."

The College Prowler Take On...
Parking

It seems to be universally advised by students that a car is both an unnecessary and expensive endeavor on BU campus, in and around the city. Not only is parking ridiculously expensive, but your car will invariably wind up towed, ticketed, abused, and worn down. The cheapest way to park is to apply for a resident permit parking pass and park on the street. All of those with cars, however, heed this warning: meter maids and towing companies are the city's most effective resources. I was towed five times ($90 a day) and received about 10 parking tickets, all within a span of three months. I was convinced that they had installed a tracking device on my car. Not only that, but I have actually taken my car with the intentions of going to class, but ended up circling the area five or six times until I was good and late, and then gave up and headed back home to bed. Sadly, this was not a one-time occurrence.

Despite the ominous nature of the parking scene described above, I admit that I did choose to have a car. The reason? It is so nice to have a quick way out of town, to head home, to a concert, a rave, or a festival. You will find that someone is always willing to pay for your gas for a ride. But then again, you might find yourself spending half of your life looking for parking. There is an advertisement that I saw in the T station that says, "The average adult spends 370 hours a year looking for parking, and 285 hours a year having sex." If that statistic is true, which it undoubtedly is, leave your car home.

The College Prowler® Grade on

Parking: D-

A high grade in this section indicates that parking is both available and affordable, and that parking enforcement isn't overly severe.

Transportation

The Lowdown On...
Transportation

Ways to Get Around Town:

On Campus

T Service
T service on the Green B Line. This line runs above ground after Kenmore Station, all the way through the center of campus. The T is $1.00 for travel inbound (toward downtown), and free for above ground service outbound. Call the MBTA for more information at (617) 222-5000.

Bus Service
Bus service on the 57 Line runs along Commonwealth Avenue from Kenmore, all the way out to Newton (this is the best mode of travel for most students who tend to live along, or off, Brighton Avenue. The bus is 75 cents each way.

Crystal Shuttle
The BU Crystal Shuttle runs back and forth from east to west campus all day. There is also the shuttle service to the dorms that are located off the main campus and to the BU Medical Campus. For more information, call the BU information desk at (617) 353-2169.

Escort Service

The BU Escort Service runs Monday to Thursday 8 p.m.-2 a.m., Friday to Sunday 8 p.m.-3 a.m. during the fall and spring semesters. Call for more information at (617) 353-4877.

Public Transportation

MBTA provides most of the public transportation in the Boston area. For more information concerning MBTA service, and other methods of travel, visit their Web site at *http://www.mbta.com*, or call (617) 222-5000.

Taxi Cabs

Brighton Cab (617) 536-0510

Checker Taxi Company (617) 536-7000

MJ Williams Company, Inc. (617) 269-6890

Red and White Cab Association (617) 242-0800

Independent Taxi Operators (617) 426-8700.

Newton Yellow Cab (617) 332-7700

Red Cab (617) 734-5000

Car Rentals

Alamo, local: (617) 561-4100; national: (800) 327-9633, *www.alamo.com*

Avis, local: (617) 534-1400; national: (800) 831-2847, *www.avis.com*

(Car Rentals continued)

Budget, local: (617)497-1800; national: (800) 527-0700, *www.budget.com*

Dollar, local: (617) 578-0025; national: (800) 800-4000. *www.dollar.com*

Enterprise, local: (617) 738-6003; national: (800) 736-8222, *www.enterprise.com*

Hertz, local: (617) 244-0801; national: (800) 654-3131, *www.hertz.com*

National, local: (617) 568-1950; national: (800) 227-7368, *www.nationalcar.com*

Best Ways to Get Around Town

MBTA service: T (operates both above and underground), Bus Lines (follows T lines around the city), MBTA rails (runs between cities around Massachusetts), biking/blading along the river, Taxi Service

Ways to Get Out of Town:

Airport

Logan International Airport, (617) 567-7844. The airport is approximately 20 minutes driving time from BU.

How to Get to the Airport

The T: Take the MBTA Blue Line to Airport Station. Free shuttle bus service is provided by MassPort from the Airport Station to all airline terminals.

(How to Get to the Airport, continued)

The bus: MBTA bus routes 448, 459, and CT3 serve Logan Airport.

By car: From Commonwealth Avenue, take Storrow Drive East, and take the exit toward 93 N/S. Follow signs to the airport.

A cab ride to the airport costs about $25.

Greyhound

The Greyhound Trailways Bus Terminal is in downtown Boston, approximately seven miles from campus

South Station
700 Atlantic Avenue
Boston, MA 02110.

For scheduling information, call (617) 526-1801.

Amtrak

There are several Amtrak Train stations located in the following areas: South Station: 700 Atlantic Avenue, Boston, MA 02110; 135 Causeway Street, at Canal Street, Boston, MA 02114; University Avenue and Route 128, Westwood, MA 02090; 145 Dartmouth Street, Boston, MA 02116. Call 1-800-USA-RAIL for all times and scheduling information, or check *http://www.amtrak.com*.

Travel Agents

The most popular travel agency used by students is STA Travel. There is one located right on campus at 738 Commonwealth Avenue. Call them at (617) 264-2030.

Did You Know?

Most methods of transportation in Boston will accept the Student Advantage Card (you will receive information about it when you arrive on campus, or during orientation). The SA card allows a 15% student discount at Amtrak and Greyhound locations.

Not-So-Fun Facts:

1. During the beginning of the war on terror, Boston was rated the second worst place to be in the country in case of an emergency.

2. The "Big Dig," Boston's enormous construction project that was originally projected to last for approximately four years, has now grown to occupy over 10 years of construction on Boston's highway system, expected finish date sometime fall of 2006.

3. When there is traffic, you could potentially be stuck at a standstill for hours before getting out of the city.

Students Speak Out On...
Transportation

> "Outside campus, it is pretty easy getting around the city on the T. The BU Green Line, which you will undoubtedly ride daily, is so slow. It is a relic that desperately needs replacing."

Q "The T is the train in Boston. It's very quick and very convenient. It gets you just about anywhere. But **the T only runs until 12:30 a.m.**, so cabs are usually the way to go after that. There is a late-night bus service, but I've never used it. It's fairly new. There are also buses that run up and down campus, so public transportation is pretty good."

Q "The T train runs right down Commonwealth Avenue where BU is located, so **it's easy to hop on the train to get anywhere** on campus. Since I lived on West Campus, I took the train to my classes, and a monthly T pass costs $44. The T stops running around midnight, so it's a pain to get home from bars and clubs and parties, but usually a bunch of people split a cab ride, and it's not so bad."

Q "**Public transportation is very accessible**. The T is near every dorm, and you can get almost everywhere on it. Commuter rails are easy to use to go out of town, and there are shuttle buses to take you to campus and back."

Q "The subway (T) runs till about 12:50 at night; after that, **it's easy to catch a cab**, and the buses are convenient, too—although you probably won't need them often."

Q "**I have found the greatest form of transportation**: it's called 'take your friend's car.'"

Q "It only costs you **$1.25 to go pretty much anywhere**. It may take you much longer then driving, but it's pretty easy to use. When you are traveling outbound and not in the tunnels, it's free. The public transit reaches everywhere throughout Boston, and the commuter rail and train station can take you anywhere you want to go. The T even goes to the airport."

Q "Walking has always been my favorite mode of travel. When the T is around, which you will find that it often isn't (especially when you are late), it's convenient. Sometimes though, **you can be waiting forever** outside Warren Towers in a snow storm and then the first two T's are either packed or don't stop!"

Q "Public transportation in Boston is awesome. It will get you virtually anywhere in town you wish to go. The only downfall is that **it can be extremely crowded, sometimes to the point where you can't even get on**."

Q "The T is slow, and it's even slower in the winter. **Here is a tip: take the bus**. Even though they aren't always going to get you to your exact destination, the transportation is much more convenient."

Q "Boston is probably the **best city in the country for transportation**. Almost every location is accessible by T within a half hour, and it's really cheap to ride. They can be crowded at times, so be early if you need to get to class. They have been known to bypass a stop, and then you must wait for the next one."

Q "Public transportation is super-convenient when it is running. Unfortunately, **the hours of operation are limited**, which means if you go off campus for a party, you may have to split a cab with friends for the way home."

The College Prowler Take On...
Transportation

Most students agree that the T is extremely simple and relatively inexpensive to ride. It runs in color-coordinated lines around and outside of the city. Almost everything is a quick T ride away, and the campus is located along the Green B Line. It is one dollar to head inbound and free coming back, as long as you stay above ground. It runs like a trolley across BU campus and can therefore get really crowded on school days. Usually, however, it is the best mode of transportation to and from class. The T stops running at 12:30 a.m., which is far from convenient, but the "Night Owl" buses continue to run until 2 a.m. on the weekends. There will be days, when it feels like it's 10 degrees below zero and you are late for a mid-term, and three different T's drive by before you are able to squeeze in. It is definitely not a good idea for claustrophobics. Reduced price passes are available each semester through BU at the student union. If you move off campus, it is a good idea to look for a place that is advertised as T-accessible. There are also free BU shuttles that travel to some of the more remote dorms. Luckily, in a bind, there are always cabs.

Pedestrians, beware! The drivers in Massachusetts, and especially in Boston, are referred to across the country as "Massholes." If you should come across an individual of this kind, run the other way. Overall, transportation in Boston is readily-accessible and easy-to-use. You definitely do not need a car. It often proves to be more of a hassle than it is worth.

B+

The College Prowler® Grade on

Transportation: B+

A high grade for Transportation indicates that campus buses, public buses, cabs, and rental cars are readily-available and affordable. Other determining factors include proximity to an airport and the necessity of transportation.

Weather

The Lowdown On...
Weather

Average Temperature:

Fall:	62 °F
Winter:	35 °F
Spring:	55 °F
Summer:	81 °F

Average Precipitation:

Fall:	3.54 in.
Winter:	3.65 in.
Spring:	3.56 in.
Summer:	3.22 in.

Students Speak Out On...
Weather

"In the fall and spring, Boston weather is really nice. However, the winters are long, cold, and often depressing. If you like cold weather and snow, then you won't mind Boston winters."

Q "If you don't like the cold, Boston is not the place for you. It gets cold around the end of October, and when I left school in May, it was just getting warm again. **It snows pretty often**, and is very windy and cold in the dead of winter."

Q **"It is kind of crappy, except for the first two months and last two months of school**, and even then it can get screwy. Basically, the winter is really cold, and it is always very windy in Boston until the summer, when it does get really nice."

Q **"The first couple of weeks and the last couple of weeks are the best!** The time in-between is cold, and there aren't many people out at all. The first couple of weeks are still warm, and people are out sitting at the BU beach and meeting with friends. But when it gets cold, most tend to stay in their dorm unless they have to venture out for food."

Q **"The weather in Boston is crazy**; there is no other way to describe how quickly it changes from sunny to rainy. But typically, there are four seasons. The weather changes drastically around October/November from kind of breezy to brisk and cold. Then from December to February, it is really freezing. It snows, sometimes a lot, sometimes a little. There are a couple of warm streaks every now and then, but it hasn't been consistent."

Q "**Boston in the fall is quite stunning**. I love the snow, because I don't get it at home, and I love bundling up and wearing coats and scarves. The wind can be a little painful sometimes, but you get used to it."

Q "Honestly, the only predictable thing about the weather is that **it is always unpredictable**. Bring lots of shorts, pants, jackets, T-shirts, everything. Layering is a good idea to help you to survive the chaotic Boston weather, which will often jump from freezing cold to humid and hot in hours!"

Q "**Boston has all four extremes of seasons**. You need everything from tank tops and shorts in the summer to down jackets, wool sweaters, and long johns in the winter. Pack heavily."

Q "**Boston is nearly unbearable in the winter**. It snows, it rains, it sleets; and while everyone likes a picturesque winter's eve once in a while, within hours of snowfall, it morphs into piles of gray and black ice lining the sides of the main streets. New England has descent skiing and boarding during the winter, though. Most ski areas in Vermont are just a couple hours away."

Q "The summer and winter in Boston are like night and day. The freezing temperatures in the winter alternate with hot and hazy days in the summer. Your best bet is to spend some cash on a **portable electric heater and window air conditioner**; it is worth the money. Dorms are extremely hot and uncomfortable during hot days, but they usually stay warm in the winter when they pump the heat. Off-campus housing usually includes heat with the monthly rent, which means that there is heat pouring into your room 24-hours a day, even when you don't need it."

Q "**The weather covers the entire temperate spectrum**, so it's safe to say that you need to pack everything. Have faith in thrift stores for anything you may forget."

Q "**Spring in Boston is beautiful**. Little white and pink flowers bloom for a few weeks during the beginning of springtime, lining the BU campus with color. Make sure you get out of the house during those days. The Boston Public Gardens are the perfect spot for studying, especially during the stressful weeks during finals."

Q "Someone once said if you don't like the weather here, wait a minute. How true! **We have everything from frigid cold to sweltering, muggy heat**, sometimes in the same day. Bring your entire wardrobe. The wind is killer; it stings your face, and chills you to the bone. Be prepared, that's the toughest thing to get used to."

Q "**The weather is erratic**. During the months from November to March, it is pretty gray and cold. Bring the warmest clothes you have . . . scarves, hats, gloves, long johns, thermals . . . all of these things you will learn to seriously love. Bring stuff that can get wet; it rains a lot, too. In fact, go ahead and bring two umbrellas . . . they break easily, bacause it is windy in Boston, as well!"

The College Prowler Take On...
Weather

Beware Seasonal Affective cases! Everyone agrees: if you like that whole warm-weather thing, stay far away from Boston. The winter weather can be brutal, and the winter always seems to creep into the fall and the spring. Most apartments have heat included, so do not make the same mistake that I did and get a place that doesn't: bills can hit $200 in the winter months. The gray skies, however, do break up occasionally, and when they do, Bostonians shed their layers and head outside. You will be amazed at how much a nice day is appreciated once you have been deprived of sunshine for so long. Boston is beautiful in the spring, once it eventually arrives.

Luckily, there are plenty of outdoor activities, depending on the weather. During the winter, the Frog Pond in the Boston Commons opens as an outdoor ice skating rink. There is also plenty of skiing and boarding nearby in neighboring states. During the warmer seasons, the Charles River provides all sorts of activities, including, sailing and boating, jogging along the water, and plenty of free outdoor music festivals. Go to the pier or to the parks for an afternoon outdoors. Of course, Boston has a million things to offer when the weather is unbearable: museums, galleries, aquarium, shopping, restaurants, theater, and clubbing.

The College Prowler® Grade on

Weather: C-

A high Weather grade designates that temperatures are mild and rarely reach extremes, that the campus tends to be sunny rather than rainy, and that weather is fairly consistent rather than unpredictable.

Report Card Summary

B+ ACADEMICS

A+ LOCAL ATMOSPHERE

B+ SAFETY & SECURITY

B+ COMPUTERS

B+ FACILITIES

A+ CAMPUS DINING

A OFF-CAMPUS DINING

D+ CAMPUS HOUSING

B+ OFF-CAMPUS HOUSING

B- DIVERSITY

C+ GUYS

B+ GIRLS

B- ATHLETICS

A- NIGHTLIFE

C GREEK LIFE

C+ DRUG SCENE

B- CAMPUS STRICTNESS

D- PARKING

B+ TRANSPORTATION

C- WEATHER

Overall Experience

Students Speak Out On...
Overall Experience

"I was wait-listed and rejected from most places, but I did get into BU with a scholarship, so I decided Boston was the place for me. I am very happy at BU—now I know everything happens for a reason."

"I love city life, and I've really enjoyed the people thus far. I'm only going to be a sophomore, but my freshman year was amazing. **If you like a city environment, there is no better place than Boston**. BU is extremely expensive, and the price goes up every year, so as long as you can afford it, I would highly recommend BU."

Q "Overall, I'm glad I'm where I'm at. I have amazing friends, and the education is the best for my major (International Relations). There are some days when everyone says they'd like to transfer because **it gets to be too much or because it gets really cold**. You doubt yourself a lot your freshman year no matter where you go. BU has some administration issues, but overall, it's livable. They're there to keep me safe, and nothing bad has ever happened to me on campus, so they're doing their job. I feel safe walking back to my dorm alone at midnight from the library. It's what you make of it; it really is. At the end of the day, it can be a hard place to meet people and make friends, but once you get a core group, you're golden. I wouldn't pass up this freshman year for anything, and I'm going back, so that should tell you something."

Q "Overall, it has been a good experience. Academically, it is challenging for me. **Some people fit in better than others**. It can be hard to find 'the real friends,' but as long as you're outgoing or, more importantly, open to meeting new people, you should be fine. I suggest that you get to know the people on your floor really well, which makes life easier. Join a club and get involved in an organization that you enjoy. This makes BU feel smaller than it really is."

Q "I like this place very much, though I still wish I could have gone to UCLA. The only thing I really regret is that we don't have a 'campus,' but aside from that, **I'm quite fond of this place**."

Q "BU is a good school and I'm glad that I go there. I love Boston completely. It's a fun city, it's clean and safe, and **it's a total college town**. I think there are about 50 colleges in the area."

Q "Overall, I have really enjoyed BU so far. Some people form a negative opinion of it based on the administrative policies like the guest policy, but there are ways around it, and hopefully it will be changed soon (there have been lots of protests about it). I have made a ton of good friends at BU, and I have gotten involved in a lot of activities such as writing a column for the student newspaper The *Daily Free Press* and writing for BUTV shows. Boston is great, and my boring town of Bloomfield, CT seems 10 times more boring after living in Boston. **There is a lot to do, and it is an exciting place to be**. I don't know what you want to major in, but the communications program at BU was one of the main reasons I went there. It is known as a really good program, and so far, I have been happy with it."

Q "I always wish I was somewhere else. But **Boston is really great for a college experience**. It isn't as big and overwhelming as New York, but it definitely isn't a small town either. You can find yourself here, or you can just look for your lost soul in vain. In any case, I am having a pleasant experience that I would exchange for nothing else than a bar of chocolate."

Q "To describe my overall experience is such a tough task. I have changed into so many different people and grew into and out of so many different phases during my four years in college. I guess the final test is whether or not I like the individual that both this school and I have created together, and I do. I did enjoy my time here, and besides the administration is a very convenient scapegoat for all of your problems, just ask the student body. **I definitely could not picture my college experience anywhere else**. And if you really do not belong here, no one has any problem leaving. More than 50 percent of my friends dropped out or transferred freshman year."

Q "I left Boston University during the fall semester of my junior year, but **BU gave me many things I carried with me the rest of my life**—a drug addiction, depression, and an overall sense of what I do not want from life. For the latter, I thank it, and for the two former, well, we all need to be challenged, right?"

Q "It was rough at first, and at the end, but the middle . . . well, it was like a sandwich, you know? Overall, **I would not choose BU if I had the choice to do it over again**, because I found the environment to be limiting for the type of person I have found myself to be. I did, however, make some amazing friends, and I wouldn't change them for the world."

Q "College was amazing for me. I had a lot of positive and negative experiences, and I wouldn't trade them for anything. **I met some of the most amazing people on the planet at BU**. I am very glad that I chose to come here. Advice: ask questions! Ask professors, advisors, upperclassmen, and kids in your classes. If you don't get answers, talk to your dean. Remember that you and your parents pay the salaries of these people, and you are entitled to know your rights as a student. Figure out all of the perks that BU life offers, like a computer lab that is open 24 hours, with $50 of printing quota per semester, and different associations that have career opportunities for your major. Think about your future, try to get involved with internships, research opportunities, or jobs that suit your interests. Remember that you are there to learn; play is secondary."

Q "**I love BU; there are great people here**. Talk to the teachers; they have connections in the field, and will help you out. You will mature here. Also, Bostonians are some of the best people in the world to know, but you have to give them a chance, and they will soon warm up. However, you must venture outside of the Commonwealth Avenue area. The area is nearly exclusively comprised of college kids that don't give an accurate representation of Boston. In fact, not going outside of the area is probably the main reason that people at BU say that they don't like Boston. They don't know it."

The College Prowler Take On...
Overall Experience

While BU certainly has its downfalls, most of which are due to the sheer size of the University, there are plenty of opportunities to take full advantage of all that it has to offer. For the resourceful and motivated individual, a little effort will go a long way. The most important thing is to utilize your professors to your advantage. It is their job to be available to their students. While some are certainly more attentive than others, students are not turned away by a professor when they have gone looking for opportunities or support.

I have tried to take full advantage of what my school has to offer. I managed to finish two majors, a 150-page senior thesis, a tutoring job, ski team, and several academic and social clubs, while maintaining freedom from campus life. Keeping busy, being well-organized, and choosing a course of study that truly stimulates your intellectual interests, will all be really helpful in having a successful experience at BU. I had dreaded graduation day for such a long time, and therefore, leaving Boston is not something that I look forward to. On the flip-side, I know countless people, many of which are close friends, who would argue the opposite perspective. Accept your environment and work with it, as well as against it. Do not stay inside for too long, and do not drink away your college years. Make school a priority, and hang out with your professors (they are the best resource you have). Boston is a huge city with a really large population of young people. If you are looking for a taste of city life, and think that you would be able to establish yourself at a big university in a high-paced atmosphere, it is definitely possible to find your niche here.

The Inside Scoop

The Lowdown On...
The Inside Scoop

BU Slang
Know the slang, know the school! Absolutely EVERYTHING is abbreviated at BU. The following is a list to help you catch on quicker:

BUCOP - BU Collaborative Degree Program

Cam-Co - Campus Convenience

CAS - College of Arts and Sciences

CFA - College of Fine Arts

CGS - College of General Studies

COM - College of Communications

ENG - College of Engineering

EOP - Center for English Language and Orientation Program (CELOP)

GMS - Graduate Medical Sciences

GRS - Graduate School of Arts and Sciences

GSM - Graduate School of Management

GSU - George Sherman Union

IT - Office of Information Technology

LAW - School of Law

MED - School of Medicine

MET - Metropolitan College

PDP - Physical Department Program

SAR - Sargent College of Health and Rehabilitation

SED - School of Education

SDM - Henry M. Goldman School of Dental Medicine

SHA - School of Hospitality Administration

SMG - School of Management

SPH - School of Public Health

SSW - School of Social Work

STH - School of Theology

SUM - Summer Term Program

UNI - University Professors

XRG - Cross Registration

Things I Wish I Knew Before Coming to BU

• The extremely high cost of living—this is especially difficult for your first taste of off-campus living.

• It is difficult to take classes in the College of Fine Arts, unless you are a minor or a major in the school, itself. I had really intended on taking some sculpture classes when I came to BU for school, yet was disappointed to learn that I had a limited selection of "classes for non-majors" to choose from, and would have been forced to take several introductory classes (like printmaking) in order to register for sculpture.

• The city closes down at 2 a.m. This is quite a culture shock, even for someone coming from a small town. I went to high school in upstate NY, and there were plenty of 24-hour diners around for late night socializing. Be prepared for early nights out, most after-hours partying takes place at off-campus apartments, or at home.

• BU is extremely conservative, especially considering the liberal student body. The former president of the University, John Silber, despite being a Democrat, seems as right-wing as they come regarding policies. When petitioning for more lenient visitation rules, students were surprised to hear this widely published response: "It is not our job to provide a 'love nest' for our students." He also disbanded the homosexual student organization at the BU Academy. This, among many other executive decisions made by those running the University, are often the spark for public controversy in the media.

Tips to Succeed at BU

• Talk to your professors. This is the number-one piece of advice for any student at BU. As I approached my senior year, I regretted the fact that I had allowed my first years at the University to slip by without getting to know my professors. Do not wait until the panic of recommendations to become your professor's best friend.

• Stay off-campus. While the University provides plenty of opportunities for meeting other students, most of my best friends, and all of my relationships, have been found during trips away from campus life. There are so many people in Boston; do not make the mistake of limiting yourself to the occasionally homogenous BU crowd.

• Use the BU Job Board. Quickie Jobs are perfect for making some easy and fast cash. BU offers its students a list of odd jobs (one-time, temporary, permanent, part-time, and full-time options) posted by people and businesses in the Boston area who are looking for help. This is a great way to make enough money to really enjoy city life. Here, money disappears frighteningly fast.

BU Urban Legends

• The third floor of the Mugar Library at BU has supposedly been rated number two in the country by *Playboy* magazine for places to pick up good-looking college girls.

• The top floor of the Photonics Building at BU (which is not accessible to students, as it requires a code for entry) is rumored to be guarded by armed security. It is said to be a federally-protected area that engages in the production of "military technology."

• It is said that if you walk across the seal on Marsh Chapel Plaza, you won't graduate.

School Spirit

BU truly lacks a strong base of students who care about university life. While there are certainly select circles that pursue the betterment of student life, it is really hard to get a good turnout at both on- and off-campus events. Occasionally the students will surprise you, but for the most part, apathy is rampant. The student response to the recent events in America has displayed the general lack of unity at BU. There were several war protests, sit-ins, teach-ins, speakers, and debates occurring on campus during that time. The attendance at most events tended to be disheartening to all those that spent hours putting them together.

Traditions

Midnight Madness
This occurs in the hockey rink at Case Athletic Center to celebrate the beginning of the season. Everyone gathers to be introduced to each player on the BU varsity team, often in a drunken frenzy.

The Beanpot Hockey Event
It occurs in the fall between
Boston University and Boston College each year, and is always a party. It's an event that is attended not only by BU students and faculty, but also by the city at large.

The Free Concert
It is "partially funded by your undergraduate student fee," (a phrase often joked about by anyone paying full tuition to attend BU), usually gets a lot of attention by students. One past act was Bob Dylan concert. Tickets were available on a first-come, first-served basis. It was incredible.

Senior Week
This happens each year during the final days between final exams and graduation. It is basically comprised of a bunch of events to which seniors and their guests may purchase discounted tickets to participate in. These include: trips to Six Flags New England, trips to the Cape, "booze-cruises" at the pier, clambakes, Boston Pops, Red Sox games, formal dances at popular Boston venues, and other events.

Finding a Job or Internship

The Lowdown On...
Finding a Job or Internship

The truth is that it is very difficult to find a "real" job in this city. Because of the high concentration of students, part-time work is not easy to come by, and to get a good job, with good pay, you really have to know someone. Your best bet is to try to find a job on campus. This will save you time, money, and effort traveling back and forth around the city. BU offers a really good service to help students find work (be it part-time, full-time, on campus or off). Check out the job board online at the Student Link at *http://www.bu.edu/studentlink*, or stop by the office on the second floor of 881 Commonwealth Avenue to get yourself oriented.

BU has a service that allows people from the community to call in and place a request for a student employee. The job opportunities are updated daily and include childcare, tutoring and teaching, administrative, clerical, internships, non-profit work, retail, food service and catering, household labor, summer jobs, recreation, and more. Sometimes the high-paying jobs are the ones that are least conducive to your academic goals, however. Do yourself a favor and find an internship or a job that will provide you with some career experience.

Grads who Enter the Job Market Within

6 Months: 65%
1 Year: 75%
2 Years: N/A

Firms That Most Frequently Hire Grads

IBM, General Electric, Mercer, Fidelity, Raytheon

Advice

It is extremely difficult to live in Boston without a fairly consistent source of funds. Unlike life in a small town, money is necessary for just about everything, and you really can't do much without it, unless you prefer quiet evenings at home . . . a lot. Those who often find themselves without cash are doomed to suffer socially. Your best bet is to get a job, even if it doesn't pay much, because a little money is better than none. When in doubt: the GSU Union Court is always hiring food service employees. You do not even have to apply if you are a BU student. The pay is minimal, but the hours are flexible, and easy to come by. Another option that is always guaranteed is the Shaw's Market on Commonwealth Avenue. It is right on campus, and they do mass hiring every Tuesday. Just show up. Most students typically find themselves working at one of the two places listed above for at least a few weeks to earn some quick cash.

Career Center Resources & Services

While the Job Board resource described above will provide you with just about all you need to know for finding a job in Boston, there is also a fully-functioning career center located in Kenmore Square at 19 Deerfield St., on the third floor. This center can be utlized for a year after levaing BU. You can call for more information at (617) 353-3590, e-mail at future@bu.edu, or visit the Web site online at *http://www.bu.edu/careers*.

Alumni

The Lowdown On...
Alumni

Web Site:
http://www.bu.edu/alumni

Office:
Alumni Relations
One Sherborn St.
Boston, MA 02215
(617) 353-9500.

Services Available
Graduates receive an Alumni Card, granting access to the following benefits at BU:

- Borrowing privileges for all circulating materials from any BU library; access to the Career Advisory Network

(Services Available, continued)

- Access to the Career Resources Library at the M.L.K. Jr. Center and other career resources and services (usually for a fee)

- A 10 percent discount at BU Dental Health Center for both alumni and dependents

- Access to a list of housing opportunities in the Greater Boston area and a list of real-estate brokers who offer discounts to BU alumni

- The opportunity for membership at Case Athletic Center

(Services Available continued)

- A 10 percent discount at Barnes & Noble at BU

- A 20 percent discount on weekend rental of the Castle for wedding receptions and/or ceremonies

- On-site access to Geddes Language Center, which supports international communications, instructional media, humanities, and videography

- Discounts for selected seminars in the Arts and in the Culinary Arts

- The opportunity to receive the BU Alumni MasterCard

- The opportunity to apply for alumni medical and life insurance at group rates

- Discounts at the Huntington Theatre Company at BU

- Opportunities to audit selected undergraduate classes at Metropolitan College (BU's night school) for $25 per credit, plus registration fees

- Half-priced parking in selected BU lots

- Use of George Sherman Union facilities

Major Alumni Events

Because alumni events vary from year to year, the best source to check is the BU Alumni Web site. Some events, for example, are BU Beer Tasting, BU at Tanglewood, Alumni Day at SAFECO Field, and the Bunches of Brunches Series. Annual events include: reunion, homecoming weekend, BU Summer Connections Nights located across the U.S., and commencement.

Alumni Publications

All alumni receive a free subscription to *Bostonia*, the major publication for BU alumni.

Alumni Club

A membership-only restaurant and event space for BU Alumni. For more info, visit *http://www.bostonuniversityclub.com*.

Did You Know?

Famous BU Alums—Martin Luther King, Jr. is certainly the most-celebrated alum from BU. Noted celebrities Howard Stern, Jason Alexander, and Bill O'Reilly have also studied at BU.

Student Organizations

There are more than 400 student organizations on campus. The following is a partial list:

African Students Organization	Cultural	buaso@bu.edu
Amnesty International	Political	amnestyi@bu.edu
Anime Group	Special Interest	buanime@bu.edu
Arab Students Association	Cultural	arabsa@bu.edu
Archaelogy Club	CAS	buarch@bu.edu
Armenian Students Association	Cultural	asa@bu.edu
Art Club	Special Interest	zone@bu.edu
Asian American Christian Fellowship	Religious	buaacf@bu.edu
Asian Baptist Student Koinonia	Religious	absk@bu.edu
Asian Student Union	Cultural	buasu@bu.edu
Aural Fixation	Performing	auralfix@bu.edu
Awareness Through the Literary Alliance of Students (ATLAS)	Special Interest	ATLAS@bu.edu
Bacchanalia	Performing	bacch@bu.edu
Baha'i Club of B.U.	Religious	bahai@bu.edu
Ballroom Dance	Performing	ballroom@bu.edu
Baptist Student Fellowship	Religious	pannpeek@bu.edu
Beit Midrash Society	Religious	bubms@bu.edu

Billiards Club	Recreation	bubc@bu.edu
Bioethics Society	CAS	tbsbu@bu.edu
Biomedical Engineers Society	ENG	bmes@bu.edu
Black Graduate & Professional Student Organization	Special Interest	bgpso@bu.edu
Bowling Association	Recreation	kingpin@bu.edu
BSBA Finance Club	SMG	bsbafin@bu.edu
BU On Tap	Performing	buontap@bu.edu
BU Television	COM	butv@bu.edu
Campus Hope	Religious	campushope@bu.edu
Cape Verdean Student Association	Cultural	cvsa@bu.edu
Caribbean Club	Cultural	b1gups@hotmail.com
CAS Forum	Govt	casforum@bu.edu
CFA Student Government	Govt	sfagov@bu.edu
Chinese Student and Scholar Association	Cultural	bucssa@bu.edu
Chinese Students Club	Cultural	buchin@bu.edu
College Bowl	Special Interest	qbowl@bu.edu
College Democrats	Political	democrat@bu.edu
College Republicans	Political	colrepub@bu.edu
Dance Theatre Group	Performing	budance@bu.edu
Danzon	Cultural	BU_Danzon@excite.com
Dear Abbeys	Performing	abbeys@bu.edu
Debate Society	Special Interest	budebate@bu.edu
Early Childhood Educators Club	SED	ecec@bu.edu
ENG Student Government	Govt	enggov@bu.edu
Enviornmental Student Organization	Community Service	eso@bu.edu
Episcopal Student Organization	Religious	episcop@bu.edu
Equestrian Team	Club Sport	buet@bu.edu
Euro-Asian &Turkish Association	Cultural	eta@bu.edu
European Business Club	MBA	ebcmba@bu.edu
Falun Gong Practice Group	Special Interest	falun@bu.edu
Figure Skating	Club Sport	bufsc@bu.edu
Filipino Student Association	Cultural	bufsa@bu.edu
Film Fest	Special Interest	filmfest@bu.edu

Film Lovers and Philosophers' Society	Special Interest	flaps@bu.edu
French Cultural Society	Cultural	fcs@bu.edu
Friends of Spartacus Youth	Political	bigalsar@bu.edu
Fundraising for Charity	Community Service	ffc@bu.edu
Gay & Lesbian Business Council	MBA	markdhue@bu.edu
German Club	CAS	BU_German @hotmail.com
Golden Key Honor Society	Honor	gknhs@bu.edu
Green Party	Political	bugreens@yahoo.com
Gymnastics Club	Club Sport	gymnasts@bu.edu
H.A.V.E. (Hunger Affects Virtually Everyone)	Community Service	have@bu.edu
Habitat for Humanity International	Community Service	habitat@bu.edu
Hawaii Cultural Association	Cultural	pauhana@bu.edu
Hellenic Association	Cultural	hellenic@bu.edu
Hindu Students Council	Religious	buhsc@bu.edu
Holocaust Education Committee	Special Interest	hoced@bu.edu
Hong Kong Student Association	Cultural	buhksa@bu.edu
Hong Kong Student Christian Fellowship	Religious	HKSCF@bu.edu
In Achord	Performing	inachord@bu.edu
In Light of This Evening's Events	Special Interest	inlightof@hotmail. com
India Club	Cultural	buic@bu.edu
Indonesian Society at Boston University	Cultural	ISABU@bu.edu
Inline Hockey Team	Club Sport	inline@bu.edu
Inner Strength Gospel Choir	Religious	isgc-1@bu.edu
Institute of Electrical & Electronics Engineers	ENG	ieee@photon. bu.edu
Inter Fraternity Sorority Council	Greek	ifsc@bu.edu
International Management Association	MBA	imabu@bu.edu
International Students Consortium	Cultural	isc@bu.edu
Intervarsity Christian Fellowship	Religious	ivcf@bu.edu
Irish American Society	Cultural	irishclb@bu.edu

Islamic Society	Religious	isbuact@bu.edu
Juggling Association	Performing	buja@bu.edu
Kappa Kappa Psi	Honor	kkpsi@bu.edu
Korean Student Association	Cultural	ksa@bu.edu
La Fuerza	Cultural	lafuerza@bu.edu
Latin American Law Student Association	LAW	lalsa@bu.edu
Latinos Unidos	Cultural	latinosu@bu.edu
Latter-day Saint Student Association	Religious	burms-list@bu.edu
Linux Users Group	Special Interest	bulug@bu.edu
Literary Society	Special Interest	clarion@bu.edu
Local Students Union	Govt	lsu@bu.edu
Lutheran Campus Ministry	Religious	lutheran@bu.edu
Marine Science Association	CAS	msa@bu.edu
Medieval Re-creation Society	Special Interest	darkages-l@bu.edu
Model United Nations	CAS	bumuna@bu.edu
Mustard Seed	Religious	seeds@bu.edu
NAACP	Political	naacp@bu.edu
National Council for International Health	SAR	ncih@bu.edu
National Society of Collegeiate Scholars	Honor	nscs@bu.edu
Navigators Christian Fellowship	Religious	navs@bu.edu
Outing Club	Recreation	outing@bu.edu
Outreach Educators for Youth Primate Alliance	Special Interest	oxfam@bu.edu
Pakistani Students Association	Cultural	pakistan@bu.edu
Phi Alpha Delta	LAW	mpettit@bu.edu
Photography Club	COM	foto@bu.edu
Pre Dental Society	CAS	pre-dent@bu.edu
Pre Medical Society	CAS	bupremed@bu.edu
Programming Council	SU	progcncl@bu.edu
R.O.C. Chinese Student Association	Cultural	roccsa@bu.edu
Real Life: Campus Crusade for Christ	Religious	reallife@bu.edu
Red Cross Volunteers	Community Service	redcross@bu.edu
Running Club	Recreation	burc@bu.edu

Russian Cultural Club	Cultural	yeralash@bu.edu
SAR: Class of 2004	Govt	gjustino@bu.edu
SHA Student Government	Govt	shagov@bu.edu
Shelter Legal Services	LAW	shelterbu@hotmail.com
Sikh Association	Religious	sikhs@bu.edu
Singapore Collegiate Society	Cultural	buscs@bu.edu
Ski Club	Special Interest	skiclub@bu.edu
Skydiving Club	Recreation	shutupandjump@bu.edu
Slow Children at Play	Performing	slowkids@bu.edu
SMG Student Government	Govt	smggovt@bu.edu
Society for Middle Eastern Studies	Cultural	mes@bu.edu
Society of Hispanic Professional Engineers	ENG	shpe@bu.edu
Society of Women Engineers	ENG	swe@bu.edu
South Campus RHA	RHA	southrha@bu.edu
Speak Easy	Community Service	speasy@bu.edu
Spectrum	Special Interest	spectrum@bu.edu
Spontaneous Combustion	Peforming	sponcom@bu.edu
SSW Student Organization	Govt	sswfed@bu.edu
Stage Troupe	Performing	stage@bu.edu
Student Union	Govt	busu@bu.edu
Taiwanese American Student Association	Cultural	tausa@bu.edu
TARANG Indian Student's Association	Cultural	tarang@bu.edu
Tau Beta Pi Association	Honor ENG	tbp@bu.edu
Tau Beta Sigma	Honor	tbsig@bu.edu
Team Learning Organization	SMG	tlo@bu.edu
Terpsichore	Performing	terps@bu.edu
Treblemakers	Performing	trebs@bu.edu
Tru Sole	Performing	bustepsq@bu.edu
Undergraduate Economics Association	CAS	ueassoc@bu.edu
Vietnamese Student Association	Cultural	buvsa@bu.edu
Warren Towers RHA	RHA	wrtrha@bu.edu
Women's Center	Special Interest	buwc@bu.edu

The Best & Worst

The Ten **BEST** Things About BU

1 The sheer size of the University allows for a huge selection of courses, from French Regional Wines (SHA HF428), to Nietzsche (CAS PH419), to Stalking the Wild Mind (UNI HU311), to Drugs and Behavior (CAS PS333), to Extragalactic Astrophysics and Cosmology (CAS AS413).

2 The professors. Allow me to put in a plug for the following professors. If you are able to take some CAS classes, do yourself a favor by seeking these individuals out. While their classes are far from an easy A, the learning experience both in the classroom, and out, was an invaluable part of my intellectual growth. Take a class with Professor Roochnik (for ancient Greek philosophy courses), Professor Griswold (for any upper level philosophy course), Professor Hasselmo (for any psychology class), and Professor Somers (for Cognitive Science).

3 Domino's Pizza takes BU Convenience Points.

4 Boston is a great college town, and the locals are highly entertaining; especially during Red Sox season.

5 There are plenty of undergraduate research opportunities (a rarity at most American colleges) for any self-motivated individual.

6 There is no Greek life. That means no ridiculous rush season, during which students at most other universities are drunk, storming the streets in single file, yelling absurdities, falling to the ground for push-ups, and swallowing goldfish, all for a chance to join and "fit-in."

7 The food, both off campus and on, is better than most other colleges.

8 West Campus cultivates that semi-campus feel.

9 The way BU beach looks at night, and the way it is reminiscent of fake scenery, which, one could argue, it is. It is the best grass on campus.

10 The intellectual atmosphere is really high at BU. This is the best environment for learning. If you are looking for more alternative methods of teaching, however, this is probably not the best thing for you.

The Ten WORST Things About BU

1 The conservative administration is an ever-present source of distress for students.

2 The size of the University makes it difficult to get to know your professors. They will not come to you. You have to put in the effort.

3 BU, like any large university, has an impenetrable bureaucracy that becomes annoyingly problematic for individual students with individual issues.

4 The security on campus is reminiscent of your seventh grade bus driver if she were to suddenly develop a thick Boston accent. Don't swipe your card more than once in the wrong direction, or you are liable to get shut out.

5 The blatant apathy of much of the student body

6 Everything is overpriced, from the housing, to the coffee, to the nightlife.

7 No smoking on campus . . . anywhere

8 We start earlier, end later, and have the least vacation time of all of the universities in the area. Also, spring break is usually one or two weeks later than the majority of colleges in the US.. This makes vacation planning with friends and family outside of BU really difficult.

9 Boston closes down at 2 a.m., with lingering party-goers until about 4 a.m. After that, you have to find your own party space.

10 Freshman classes at BU tend to feel like a waste of time. Most of the quality professors never teach them, and they are usually filled beyond the maximum and held in a large auditorium. Not only that, but many of these introductory classes have weekly discussion sections that cut into and complicate scheduling when registering for classes.

Visiting

The Lowdown On...
Visiting

Hotel Information:

While there are innumerable places to stay in Boston, this is a list of accommodations that are closest and most convenient when visiting the Charles River campus. Keep in mind that rates vary based on season. The rates provided below serve as an example of the typical rates per night in September for a single/double room:

Hotel Commonwealth
500 Commonwealth Avenue
Boston, MA 02215

(866) 784-4000

www.hotelcommonwealth.com

Distance from Campus: Less than one mile

Price Range: $179–$200

➡

The Eliot

370 Commonwealth Avenue
Boston, MA 02215

(800) 44ELIOT

www.eliothotel.com

Distance from Campus:
Less than two miles

Price Range: $195–$235

Hyatt Regency Cambridge

575 Memorial Drive
Cambridge, MA 02139

(617) 492-1234

http://www.cambridge.hyatt.com

Distance from Campus:
Less than one mile

Price Range: $179 and up

Marriott Courtyard Boston Brookline

40 Webster Street
Brookline, MA 02446

(617) 734-1393

www.brooklinecourtyard.com

Distance from Campus:
Less than three miles

Price Range: $129–$229

Park Plaza Hotel

64 Arlington Street
Boston, MA 02116

(617) 426-2000

www.bostonparkplaza.com

Distance from Campus:
Less than five miles

Price Range: $179–$209

DoubleTree Guest Suites Hotel

400 Soldiers Field Road
Boston, MA 02134-1893

(617) 783-0090

www.doubletree.com

Distance from Campus:
Less than five miles

Price Range: $170 and up

Holiday Inn Boston at Brookline

1200 Beacon Street
Brookline, MA 02446

(617) 277-1200

www.holidayinnboston.com/hotels/bklma.html

Distance from Campus:
Less than three miles

Price Range: $159–$199

Marriott Copley Place

110 Huntington Avenue
Boston, MA 02116

(617) 236-5800

www.marriott.com

Distance from Campus:
Less than three miles

Price Range: $139–$179

Omni Parker House
60 School Street
Boston, MA 02108
(617) 227-8600
www.omnihotels.com
Distance from Campus:
Less than four miles
Price Range: $149–$199

Sheraton Boston
39 Dalton Street
Boston, MA 02199
(617) 236-2000
www.sheraton.com/boston
Distance from campus:
Less than five miles
Price Range: $129–$159

Take a Campus Virtual Tour

Go to *http://www.bu.edu/visit/tours/index.html*. You can also reach this site by going to *http://www.bu.edu*, clicking on "admissions," and checking out the "visitor center" option. There is a self-directed tour, as well as a virtual tour available at that site.

To Schedule a Group Information Session or Interview

Contact the Office of Admissions at:
121 Bay State Road
Boston, MA 02215
(617) 353-2300
E-mail: visit@bu.edu

Campus Tours

Tours of the Charles River campus depart from the Admissions Reception Center, 121 Bay State Road. Join an information session for prospective students, and take a student-guided tour of campus. You can also arrange in advance to sit in on a class (academic year only), have lunch with a student in a dining hall, and visit with a faculty member and academic advisors at any of the schools and colleges. You can schedule any of these events on the online Admissions Calendar on the BU Web site, where you can create a personal itinerary for your visit, or by calling (617) 353-9815 at least two weeks in advance.

Directions to Campus

Driving from the North

Travel South on Route 95 to Route 93. Take Exit 26-A to the Leverett Connector Bridge and exit directly onto Storrow Drive westbound to the Kenmore Square Exit (left exit). Use the right-hand side of the exit ramp for Kenmore Square. Turn right at the light at the end of the exit ramp. Stay to the right to remain on Bay State Road. The Reception Center will be on the right, at 121 Bay State Road.

Driving from the South

Take Route 93 North to Exit 26 (Storrow Drive/Back Bay). Go West on Storrow Drive to the Kenmore Square Exit (left exit). Use the right-hand side of the exit ramp for Kenmore Square. Turn right at the light at the end of the exit ramp. Stay to the right to remain on Bay State Road. The Reception Center will be on the right, at 121 Bay State Road.

Driving from the East

You won't be coming from the East . . . unless you are planning on swimming across the Atlantic to arrive at BU. If that is the case, then your dedication is extremely admirable, and you will have no problem finding your own directions.

Driving from the West

Take the Massachusetts Turnpike (I-90) to Exit 18 (Cambridge/ Brighton). Pay the one dollar toll, and then follow the signs for Cambridge through the first light. Turn right at the next light, keeping the Doubletree Guest Suites Hotel on the right. Take the Soldiers Field Road/Storrow Drive to the Kenmore Square exit to the Kenmore Square Exit (left exit). Use the right-hand side of the exit ramp for Kenmore Square. Turn right at the light at the end of the exit ramp. Stay to the right to remain on Bay State Road. The Reception Center will be on the right, at 121 Bay State Road.

Planning to Visit Boston?

Still trying to figure it all out? If you need some extra guidance, a campus visit can help you get acquainted. Whether it's just shopping around for colleges, or to learn more about the city known as "America's College Town," **www.bostonvisit.com** is a great place to start.

- Free Trip Planning Assistance
- Online Driving Directions
- Hotel Reservations and Discounts
- Information on Area Colleges
- Amtrak Discounts
- Recommendations, Maps, and More.

Come see for yourself.

Online at **www.bostonvisit.com** or call (888) 99-VISIT for more info.

The Charles Hotel

The Charles Hotel is located in the heart of Harvard Square. It's newly renovated and combines classic New England design with sophisticated luxury service. Features include multiple fine dining options— including Henrietta's Table, a jazz club, and ice skating rink. It's close to Harvard, Lesley, MIT, and BU.

Check it out . . . and ask for the Campus Visit rate.

www.charleshotel.com

Campus Visit ® Travel Desk

Want free assistance planning your visit to Boston-area colleges and universities? Call (888) 99-VISIT. You can chat with a live consultant about travel arrangements, hotel discounts, directions, and more. Or check out *www.bostonvisit.com*.

Traveling by train?

Check out Amtrak's two-for-one discount on *www.campusvisit.com/ amtrak*. Buy a ticket for a campus visit and your parent/guardian travels free. With more than 500 destinations, you can visit almost any campus in the US.

Miles & Minutes to Local Campuses
Boston University to...

Bentley College	9.5 miles; 27 minutes
Berklee College of Music	1.1 miles; 9 minutes
Boston Conservatory	0.9 miles; 8 minutes
Brandeis University	12.9 miles; 21 minutes
Emerson College	2.1 miles; 10 minutes
Emmanuel College	1.2 miles; 9 minutes
Harvard University	3.5 miles; 14 minutes
MIT	1.3 miles; 10 minutes
Merrimack College	26.5 miles; 43 minutes
Mount Ida College	6.9 miles; 22 minutes
Northeastern University	1.7 miles; 12 minutes
School of the Museum of Fine Arts (SMFA)	1.3 miles; 5 minutes
Stonehill College	27.1 miles; 42 minutes
Suffolk University	2.6 miles; 12 minutes
Tufts University	5.8 miles; 21 minutes
Wellesley College	12.3 miles; 30 minutes
Wheaton College	41.3 miles; 55 minutes

Words to Know

Academic Probation – A suspension imposed on a student if he or she fails to keep up with the school's minimum academic requirements. Those unable to improve their grades after receiving this warning can face dismissal.

Beer Pong / Beirut – A drinking game involving cups of beer arranged in a pyramid shape on each side of a table. The goal is to get a ping pong ball into one of the opponent's cups by throwing the ball or hitting it with a paddle. If the ball lands in a cup, the opponent is required to drink the beer.

Bid – An invitation from a fraternity or sorority to 'pledge' (join) that specific house.

Blue-Light Phone – Brightly-colored phone posts with a blue light bulb on top. These phones exist for security purposes and are located at various outside locations around most campuses. In an emergency, a student can pick up one of these phones (free of charge) to connect with campus police or a security escort.

Campus Police – Police who are specifically assigned to a given institution. Campus police are typically not regular city officers; they are employed by the university in a full-time capacity.

Club Sports – A level of sports that falls somewhere between varsity and intramural. If a student is unable to commit to a varsity team but has a lot of passion for athletics, a club sport could be a better, less intense option. Even less demanding, intramural (IM) sports often involve no traveling and considerably less time.

Cocaine – An illegal drug. Also known as "coke" or "blow," cocaine often resembles a white crystalline or powdery substance. It is highly addictive and dangerous.

Common Application – An application with which students can apply to multiple schools.

Course Registration – The period of official class selection for the upcoming quarter or semester. Prior to registration, it is best to prepare several back-up courses in case a particular class becomes full. If a course is full, students can place themselves on the waitlist, although this still does not guarantee entry.

Division Athletics – Athletic classifications range from Division I to Division III. Division IA is the most competitive, while Division III is considered to be the least competitive.

Dorm – A dorm (or dormitory) is an on-campus housing facility. Dorms can provide a range of options from suite-style rooms to more communal options that include shared bathrooms. Most first-year students live in dorms. Some upperclassmen who wish to stay on campus also choose this option.

Early Action – An application option with which a student can apply to a school and receive an early acceptance response without a binding commitment. This system is becoming less and less available.

Early Decision – An application option that students should use only if they are certain they plan to attend the school in question. If a student applies using the early decision option and is admitted, he or she is required and bound to attend that university. Admission rates are usually higher among students who apply through early decision, as the student is clearly indicating that the school is his or her first choice.

Ecstasy – An illegal drug. Also known as "E" or "X," ecstasy looks like a pill and most resembles an aspirin. Considered a party drug, ecstasy is very dangerous and can be deadly.

Ethernet – An extremely fast Internet connection available in most university-owned residence halls. To use an Ethernet connection properly, a student will need a network card and cable for his or her computer.

Fake ID – A counterfeit identification card that contains false information. Most commonly, students get fake IDs with altered birthdates so that they appear to be older than 21 (and therefore of legal drinking age). Even though it is illegal, many college students have fake IDs in hopes of purchasing alcohol or getting into bars.

Frosh – Slang for "freshman" or "freshmen."

Hazing – Initiation rituals administered by some fraternities or sororities as part of the pledging process. Many universities have outlawed hazing due to its degrading and sometimes dangerous nature.

Intramurals (IMs) – A popular, and usually free, sport league in which students create teams and compete against one another. These sports vary in competitiveness and can include a range of activities—everything from billiards to water polo. IM sports are a great way to meet people with similar interests.

Keg – Officially called a half-barrel, a keg contains roughly 200 12-ounce servings of beer.

LSD – An illegal drug. Also known as acid, this hallucinogenic drug most commonly resembles a tab of paper.

Marijuana – An illegal drug. Also known as weed or pot; along with alcohol, marijuana is one of the most commonly-found drugs on campuses across the country.

Major –The focal point of a student's college studies; a specific topic that is studied for a degree. Examples of majors include physics, English, history, computer science, economics, business, and music. Many students decide on a specific major before arriving on campus, while others are simply "undecided" until delcaring a major. Those who are extremely interested in two areas can also choose to double major.

Meal Block – The equivalent of one meal. Students on a meal plan usually receive a fixed number of meals per week. Each meal, or "block," can be redeemed at the school's dining facilities in place of cash. Often, a student's weekly allotment of meal blocks will be forfeited if not used.

Minor – An additional focal point in a student's education. Often serving as a complement or addition to a student's main area of focus, a minor has fewer requirements and prerequisites to fulfill than a major. Minors are not required for graduation from most schools; however some students who want to explore many different interests choose to pursue both a major and a minor.

Mushrooms – An illegal drug. Also known as "'shrooms," this drug resembles regular mushrooms but is extremely hallucinogenic.

Off-Campus Housing – Housing from a particular landlord or rental group that is not affiliated with the university. Depending on the college, off-campus housing can range from extremely popular to non-existent. Students who choose to live off campus are typically given more freedom, but they also have to deal with possible subletting scenarios, furniture, bills, and other issues. In addition to these factors, rental prices and distance often affect a student's decision to move off campus.

Office Hours – Time that teachers set aside for students who have questions about coursework. Office hours are a good forum for students to go over any problems and to show interest in the subject material.

Pledging – The early phase of joining a fraternity or sorority, pledging takes place after a student has gone through rush and received a bid. Pledging usually lasts between one and two semesters. Once the pledging period is complete and a particular student has done everything that is required to become a member, that student is considered a brother or sister. If a fraternity or a sorority would decide to "haze" a group of students, this initiation would take place during the pledging period.

Private Institution – A school that does not use tax revenue to subsidize education costs. Private schools typically cost more than public schools and are usually smaller.

Prof – Slang for "professor."

Public Institution – A school that uses tax revenue to subsidize education costs. Public schools are often a good value for in-state residents and tend to be larger than most private colleges.

Quarter System (or Trimester System) – A type of academic calendar system. In this setup, students take classes for three academic periods. The first quarter usually starts in late September or early October and concludes right before Christmas. The second quarter usually starts around early to mid–January and finishes up around March or April. The last academic quarter, or "third quarter," usually starts in late March or early April and finishes up in late May or Mid-June. The fourth quarter is summer. The major difference between the quarter system and semester system is that students take more, less comprehensive courses under the quarter calendar.

RA (Resident Assistant) – A student leader who is assigned to a particular floor in a dormitory in order to help to the other students who live there. An RA's duties include ensuring student safety and providing assistance wherever possible.

Recitation – An extension of a specific course; a review session. Some classes, particularly large lectures, are supplemented with mandatory recitation sessions that provide a relatively personal class setting.

Rolling Admissions – A form of admissions. Most commonly found at public institutions, schools with this type of policy continue to accept students throughout the year until their class sizes are met. For example, some schools begin accepting students as early as December and will continue to do so until April or May.

Room and Board – This figure is typically the combined cost of a university-owned room and a meal plan.

Room Draw/Housing Lottery – A common way to pick on-campus room assignments for the following year. If a student decides to remain in university-owned housing, he or she is assigned a unique number that, along with seniority, is used to determine his or her housing for the next year.

Rush – The period in which students can meet the brothers and sisters of a particular chapter and find out if a given fraternity or sorority is right for them. Rushing a fraternity or a sorority is not a requirement at any school. The goal of rush is to give students who are serious about pledging a feel for what to expect.

Semester System – The most common type of academic calendar system at college campuses. This setup typically includes two semesters in a given school year. The fall semester starts around the end of August or early September and concludes before winter vacation. The spring semester usually starts in mid-January and ends in late April or May.

Student Center/Rec Center/Student Union – A common area on campus that often contains study areas, recreation facilities, and eateries. This building is often a good place to meet up with fellow students; depending on the school, the student center can have a huge role or a non-existent role in campus life.

Student ID – A university-issued photo ID that serves as a student's key to school-related functions. Some schools require students to show these cards in order to get into dorms, libraries, cafeterias, and other facilities. In addition to storing meal plan information, in some cases, a student ID can actually work as a debit card and allow students to purchase things from bookstores or local shops.

Suite – A type of dorm room. Unlike dorms that feature communal bathrooms shared by the entire floor, suites offer bathrooms shared only among the suite. Suite-style dorm rooms can house anywhere from two to ten students.

TA (Teacher's Assistant) – An undergraduate or grad student who helps in some manner with a specific course. In some cases, a TA will teach a class, assist a professor, grade assignments, or conduct office hours.

Undergraduate – A student in the process of studying for his or her bachelor's degree.

ABOUT THE AUTHOR

I certainly hope that this information, as well as my various personal experiences, have been at least somewhat useful in your decision-making process in choosing a school. The truth is, while being prepared and advised is extremely beneficial, the best way to check out BU is to check out BU. Come visit and hang out on your own for a bit. As soon as I arrived on campus, I felt comfortable and confident that I could be both happy and productive in this environment. This does not mean, however, that it will feel the same to you.

So, what am I going to do now? Right after graduation, and the completion of my thesis, I moved to LA for about eight months. I had planned to do some quality "finding myself" time—but spent most of it partying and hanging out in the desert. It was around the time that I felt my brain was atrophying that I decided to return to the East Coast. I am now working as a research assistant and study coordinator in the neuroscience department at MGH (a part of Harvard Medical School).

I am planning to hit up NYC for graduate school, but I have yet to decide on a direction for study. I intend to get my PhD in something, perhaps evolutionary psychology, philosophy of mind, or cognition studies. I don't know. Remember, no matter how many friends, relatives, and complete strangers look at you and say, "So, what are you going to do?" it is okay to have no idea. I still don't. My long-term plan is to remain in an academic environment for a while. As long as my parents keep paying, I will keep going . . . indefinitely. I suggest you do the same. Do not rush into the mechanism. Feed your head.

I would like to thank the people at College Prowler for all of their help through this process, all of those at BU who offered their insight for the creation of this book, and anyone else who has provided me with little nuggets of wisdom. If you have any questions, need to talk, or if you suddenly engage in a personal revelation concerning the nature of the self and its relation to the physical world, don't hesitate to e-mail me at carenwalker@collegeprowler.com. Good Luck!

Caren M. Walker

The College Prowler Big Book of Colleges

Having Trouble Narrowing Down Your Choices?

Try Going Bigger!

BIG BOOK OF COLLEGES '08
7¼" X 10", 1106 Pages Paperback
$29.95 Retail
1-4274-0001-6

Choosing the perfect school can be an overwhelming challenge. Luckily, our *Big Book of Colleges* makes that task a little less daunting. We've packed it with overviews of our full library of single-school guides— nearly 250 of the nation's top schools—giving you some much-needed perspective on your search.

College Prowler on the Web

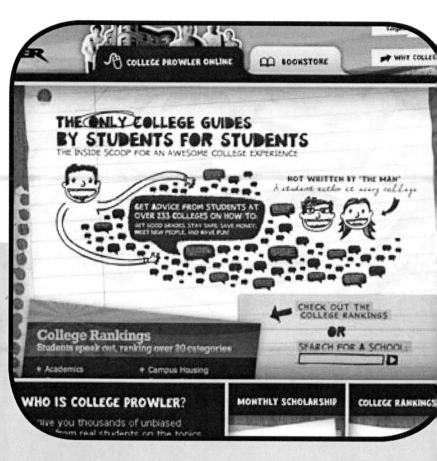

Craving some electronic interaction? Check out the new and improved **CollegeProwler.com**! We've included the COMPLETE contents of all 250 of our single-school guides on the Web—and you can gain access to all of them for just $39.95 per year!

Not only that, but non-subscribers can still view and compare our grades for each school, order books at our online bookstore, or enter our monthly scholarship contest. Don't get left in the dark when making your college decision. Let College Prowler be your guide!

Get the Hookup!

College Prowler Hookup gives you a peek behind the scenes

The Hookup is our new blog designed to hook you up with great information, funny videos, cool contests, awesome scholarship opportunities, and honest insight into who we are and what we're all about.

Check us out at ***www.collegeprowlerhookup.com***

Need Help Paying For School?

Apply for our scholarship!

College Prowler awards thousands of dollars a year
to students who compose the best essays.
E-mail scholarship@collegeprowler.com for more
information, or call 1-800-290-2682.

Apply now at ***www.collegeprowler.com***

Tell Us What Life Is Really Like at Your School!

Have you ever wanted to let people know what your college is really like? Now's your chance to help millions of high school students choose the right college.

Let your voice be heard.

Check out *www.collegeprowler.com* for more info!

Need More Help?

Do you have more questions about this school? Can't find a certain statistic? College Prowler is here to help. We are the best source of college information out there. We have a network of thousands of students who can get the latest information on any school to you ASAP. E-mail us at info@collegeprowler.com with your college-related questions.

E-Mail Us Your College-Related Questions!

Check out *www.collegeprowler.com* for more details.
1-800-290-2682

Write For Us!
Get published! Voice your opinion.

Writing a College Prowler guidebook is both fun and rewarding; our open-ended format allows your own creativity free reign. Our writers have been featured in national newspapers and have seen their names in bookstores across the country. Now is your chance to break into the publishing industry with one of the country's fastest-growing publishers!

Apply now at ***www.collegeprowler.com***

Contact editor@collegeprowler.com or
call 1-800-290-2682 for more details.

Pros and Cons

Still can't figure out if this is the right school for you?
You've already read through this in-depth guide; why not
list the pros and cons? It will really help with narrowing down
your decision and determining whether or not
this school is right for you.

Pros	Cons
....	....
....	....
....	....
....	....
....	....
....	....
....	....
....	....
....	....
....	....
....	....
....	....
....	....

Pros and Cons

Still can't figure out if this is the right school for you?
You've already read through this in-depth guide; why not
list the pros and cons? It will really help with narrowing down
your decision and determining whether or not
this school is right for you.

Pros	Cons
....	....
....	....
....	....
....	....
....	....
....	....
....	....
....	....
....	....
....	....
....	....
....	....
....	....

Notes

....

....

....

....

....

....

....

....

....

....

....

....

....

....

Notes

....

....

....

....

....

....

....

....

....

....

....

....

....

Notes

....

....

....

....

....

....

....

....

....

....

....

....

....

Notes

....

....

....

....

....

....

....

....

....

....

....

....

....

Notes

....

....

....

....

....

....

....

....

....

....

....

....

....

Notes

....

....

....

....

....

....

....

....

....

....

....

....

....

COLLEGE PROWLER®

Order now! • *collegeprowler.com* • 1.800.290.2682
Over 260 single-school guidebooks!

Albion College
Alfred University
Allegheny College
American University
Amherst College
Arizona State University
Auburn University
Babson College
Ball State University
Bard College
Barnard College
Bates College
Baylor University
Beloit College
Bentley College
Binghamton University
Birmingham Southern College
Boston College
Boston University
Bowdoin College
Brandeis University
Brigham Young University
Brown University
Bryn Mawr College
Bucknell University
Cal Poly
Cal Poly Pomona
Cal State Northridge
Cal State Sacramento
Caltech
Carleton College
Carnegie Mellon University
Case Western Reserve
Centenary College of Louisiana
Centre College
Claremont McKenna College
Clark Atlanta University
Clark University
Clemson University
Colby College
Colgate University
College of Charleston
College of the Holy Cross
College of William & Mary
College of Wooster
Colorado College
Columbia University
Connecticut College
Cornell University
Creighton University
CUNY Hunters College
Dartmouth College
Davidson College
Denison University
DePauw University
Dickinson College
Drexel University
Duke University
Duquesne University
Earlham College
East Carolina University
Elon University
Emerson College
Emory University
FIT
Florida State University
Fordham University

Franklin & Marshall College
Furman University
Geneva College
George Washington University
Georgetown University
Georgia Tech
Gettysburg College
Gonzaga University
Goucher College
Grinnell College
Grove City College
Guilford College
Gustavus Adolphus College
Hamilton College
Hampshire College
Hampton University
Hanover College
Harvard University
Harvey Mudd College
Haverford College
Hofstra University
Hollins University
Howard University
Idaho State University
Illinois State University
Illinois Wesleyan University
Indiana University
Iowa State University
Ithaca College
IUPUI
James Madison University
Johns Hopkins University
Juniata College
Kansas State
Kent State University
Kenyon College
Lafayette College
LaRoche College
Lawrence University
Lehigh University
Lewis & Clark College
Louisiana State University
Loyola College in Maryland
Loyola Marymount University
Loyola University Chicago
Loyola University New Orleans
Macalester College
Marlboro College
Marquette University
McGill University
Miami University of Ohio
Michigan State University
Middle Tennessee State
Middlebury College
Millsaps College
MIT
Montana State University
Mount Holyoke College
Muhlenberg College
New York University
North Carolina State
Northeastern University
Northern Arizona University
Northern Illinois University
Northwestern University
Oberlin College
Occidental College

Ohio State University
Ohio University
Ohio Wesleyan University
Old Dominion University
Penn State University
Pepperdine University
Pitzer College
Pomona College
Princeton University
Providence College
Purdue University
Reed College
Rensselaer Polytechnic Institute
Rhode Island School of Design
Rhodes College
Rice University
Rochester Institute of Technology
Rollins College
Rutgers University
San Diego State University
Santa Clara University
Sarah Lawrence College
Scripps College
Seattle University
Seton Hall University
Simmons College
Skidmore College
Slippery Rock
Smith College
Southern Methodist University
Southwestern University
Spelman College
St. Joseph's University Phillabelphia
St. John's University
St. Louis University
St. Olaf College
Stanford University
Stetson University
Stony Brook University
Susquahanna University
Swarthmore College
Syracuse University
Temple University
Tennessee State University
Texas A & M University
Texas Christian University
Towson University
Trinity College Connecticut
Trinity University Texas
Truman State
Tufts University
Tulane University
UC Berkeley
UC Davis
UC Irvine
UC Riverside
UC San Diego
UC Santa Barbara
UC Santa Cruz
UCLA
Union College
University at Albany
University at Buffalo
University of Alabama
University of Arizona
University of Central Florida
University of Chicago

University of Colorado
University of Connecticut
University of Delaware
University of Denver
University of Florida
University of Georgia
University of Illinois
University of Iowa
University of Kansas
University of Kentucky
University of Maine
University of Maryland
University of Massachusetts
University of Miami
University of Michigan
University of Minnesota
University of Mississippi
University of Missouri
University of Nebraska
University of New Hampshire
University of North Carolina
University of Notre Dame
University of Oklahoma
University of Oregon
University of Pennsylvania
University of Pittsburgh
University of Puget Sound
University of Rhode Island
University of Richmond
University of Rochester
University of San Diego
University of San Francisco
University of South Carolina
University of South Dakota
University of South Florida
University of Southern California
University of Tennessee
University of Texas
University of Utah
University of Vermont
University of Virginia
University of Washington
University of Wisconsin
UNLV
Ursinus College
Valparaiso University
Vanderbilt University
Vassar College
Villanova University
Virginia Tech
Wake Forest University
Warren Wilson College
Washington and Lee University
Washington University in St. Louis
Wellesley College
Wesleyan University
West Point
West Virginia University
Wheaton College IL
Wheaton College MA
Whitman College
Wilkes University
Williams College
Xavier University
Yale University